Steve Parish
AUSTRALIA GUIDE

STATE BY STATE COVERAGE WITH SUPERB PHOTOGRAPHS

CONTENTS

Once, many years ago when I was a naive young adventurer, I thought that the best way to travel was look at a map, set a schedule and stick to it, no matter what the distractions along the way. After some years of this, I went to the opposite extreme, and wandered Australia without too many fixed objectives and without much of a timetable either. I looked at the landscape as I travelled, and stopped at likely places for as long as it took me to record images of the sights I saw and the people I met.

Today, like most people who open this book, I travel with limited time and on a set budget, and I can rarely spare as much time as I would like to spend at special places. So I take photographs as I go, and, when I reach home and view the images I have taken, I have the pleasure of discovering my favourite places all over again.

The Australia Guide is the book I wish had been available when I was planning my first expedition all those years ago. It showcases the highlights of Australia's cities, rural lands, national parks and outback, describing their locations and attractions in pictures and words.

I hope that this book will help you to plan your trip to many exciting parts of our wonderful country, and that it will serve to refresh your memories of your adventure when you are safely home once again.

Steve Parish

ABOUT AUSTRALIA

Australia has many natural wonders and some of the world's loveliest cities. There are great beaches and fine national parks that everyone can use. It is a safe, easy and healthy country in which to travel, and Australians are friendly people who make visitors, whether local or from overseas, feel welcome.

FACTS ABOUT AUSTRALIA

Area (including Tasmania) ....7 682 300 sq km
Total length of coastline..........................approx. 36 735 km
Distance north–south.................................approx. 3680 km
Distance east–west......................................approx. 4000 km
Highest point.......................................Mt Kosciuszko 2228 m
Areas of Australian States and mainland Territories:
  New South Wales....................................801 600 sq km
  Victoria ....227 600 sq km
  Tasmania ....67 800 sq km
  South Australia ....984 000 sq km
  Western Australia..................................2 525 500 sq km
  Queensland ....1 727 200 sq km
  Australian Capital Territory ....2 400 sq km
  Northern Territory....................................1 346 200 sq km
Australian Time Zones
  Eastern Standard Time ....10 hrs ahead of UT*
    Qld, NSW, ACT, Vic, Tas
  Central Standard Time ....9.5 hrs ahead of UT*
    SA, NT, Broken Hill/W. NSW
  Western Australian Standard Time .....8 hrs ahead of UT*

All States except Qld and WA adopt daylight saving time
(1 hour) from last Sunday in October to last in Sunday March.

* UT (Universal Time) was GMT (Greenwich Mean Time)

FACTS ABOUT AUSTRALIANS

Today there are more than 18 million Australians. More than 20% of Australians were born overseas, more than 75% are of European (mainly British) origins, and there are significant numbers of people of Asian-Pacific backgrounds.

There have been Aboriginal, or indigenous, Australians on the continent for at least 75 000 years. Although today indigenous people (Aborigines and Torres Strait Islanders) are relatively few in numbers, they are active members of society and influential in Australia's cultural identity.

Well over half of today's Australians live within one hour's drive of the eastern seaboard of the continent, from Queensland to South Australia. There is another, smaller concentration of population in the south-west corner of Western Australia.

English is the language most often spoken in Australia, but the multicultural nature of society, especially in cities and larger towns, means that interpreters for overseas visitors with little or no English are not difficult to find. Many indigenous Australians speak one or more dialects of various Aboriginal languages as well as English.

The great monoliths of Kata Tjuta, considered by some to be even more impressive than Uluru, in Australia's Red Centre.

It is difficult for overseas visitors to imagine the sheer size of the Australian continent. Even Australians sometimes find it hard to grasp the enormous distance between Darwin and Adelaide, or between Perth and Sydney, or between Alice Springs and anywhere on the coastline. Modern methods of transport have reduced greatly times spent in transit, but the down side of such efficiency is that whereas earlier travellers had the time to see and savour the scenery on a journey, today, all too often, it flashes by car or train in a blur, or lies unseen thousands of metres below the aircraft. A leisurely pace will yield great rewards.

Rainforests are found in eastern Australia's high rainfall areas.

THE OUTBACK

The outback is the name often given to the rural areas of Australia, especially the pastoral country which is sparsely populated and where roads, except for major highways, are usually unsealed. Family sedans can go most places in Australia when the weather is reasonable, but for mud, flood, dust, sand or snow, a four-wheel drive is preferable. Any unsealed route, especially if shown on a map as a "track" (e.g. Birdsville Track or Tanami Track) or a "developmental road" may have stretches which become impassible after heavy rain. Travellers who explore the outback by car or motor bike soon become wary of speeding along unfenced roads, especially between 5 p.m. and 8 a.m. Late afternoon to mid-morning is when kangaroos, sheep and cattle wander the road verges in search of something to eat. In some areas birds of prey may scavenge road-kills, creating another hazard for motorists.

AUSTRALIA'S PHYSICAL FEATURES

From east to west, Australia can roughly be divided into four major landforms:
- A narrow coastal strip of fertile, well-watered country, with many rivers and harbours. This contains most of the largest cities and towns.
- The Great Dividing Range, a line of highlands running from Cape York down to Tasmania and across southern Victoria to South Australia. Most of Australia's remaining rainforest is found here, as well as the continent's alpine areas.
- A series of shallow basins. The northern area, Queensland's Channel Country, is drained by rivers into usually-dry Lake Eyre (15 m below sea-level) in South Australia. The southern area is drained by the Murray-Darling River system.
- The dry Western Plateau, which covers most of the western half of the continent and lies between 300 and 600 m above sea-level. From this rise the weathered stumps of once-enormous mountains, such as the MacDonnell and Musgrave Ranges in central Australia.

The Great Barrier Reef stretches for 2000 km from Torres Strait southwards down the coast of Queensland.

The flow of the Murray, Australia's longest river, is impeded near the towns of Albury and Wodonga to form Lake Hume.

An aerial view of Central Australia's famous landmarks, Uluru and, in the distance, Kata Tjuta.

The Australian Alps, in south-eastern Australia, are the highest part of the Great Dividing Range.

The Top End of the Northern Territory in the Wet.

Arid landscape, central Australia.

Winter in the Australian Alps, Victoria.

A DIVERSITY OF CLIMATES

Australia's seasons are the reverse of those in the Northern Hemisphere and temperatures and rainfall differ widely from north to south of the continent (*see table, right*). Some parts of Australia have four distinct seasons, but in some they are less distinct. Generally speaking, it rains in winter in the south, and in summer in the north. Rainfall decreases as distance from the coast increases, and there are vast interior aridlands. Road travel in southern Australia (except for alpine roads, which may be closed temporarily by heavy snowfalls) is possible all year round. Travel in northern Australia may be limited after the summer monsoon known as the "Wet" begins and rivers become flooded.

ANNUAL AVERAGE TEMPERATURES AND RAINFALL FOR THREE REGIONS

TOP END NT	J	F	M	A	M	J	J	A	S	O	N	D
MAXIMUM °C	32	31	32	33	32	31	30	31	32	33	33	33
MINIMUM °C	25	25	24	24	22	20	19	21	23	25	25	25
RAINFALL mm	406	349	311	97	21	1	1	7	19	74	143	232
CENTRAL AUSTRALIA	J	F	M	A	M	J	J	A	S	O	N	D
MAXIMUM °C	36	35	32	28	23	20	19	22	27	31	33	35
MINIMUM °C	21	21	17	13	8	5	4	6	10	15	18	20
RAINFALL mm	36	42	37	14	17	15	16	12	9	21	26	37
VIC. ALPS	J	F	M	A	M	J	J	A	S	O	N	D
MAXIMUM °C	18	19	15	10	6	3	1	3	5	9	13	15
MINIMUM °C	8	9	7	4	1	-2	-4	-2	-1	1	4	5
RAINFALL mm	88	59	121	154	195	175	266	256	210	179	168	172

WILDLIFE FOR TRAVELLERS

Red-eyed Tree-frog.

Australia's native birds and reptiles are easiest to see during the day, while mammals and frogs emerge to feed at night. However, there are plenty of excellent zoos and nature sanctuaries where native animals can be viewed closeup, and many have special facilities for seeing nocturnal animals. Australia does have some venomous snakes and spiders, and the Saltwater Crocodile and marine stingers pose dangers on beaches and in estuaries and rivers around northern coasts. The wise traveller avoids any contact with such creatures.

Laughing Kookaburra.

Red Kangaroos.

Common Wombat.

Green Python.

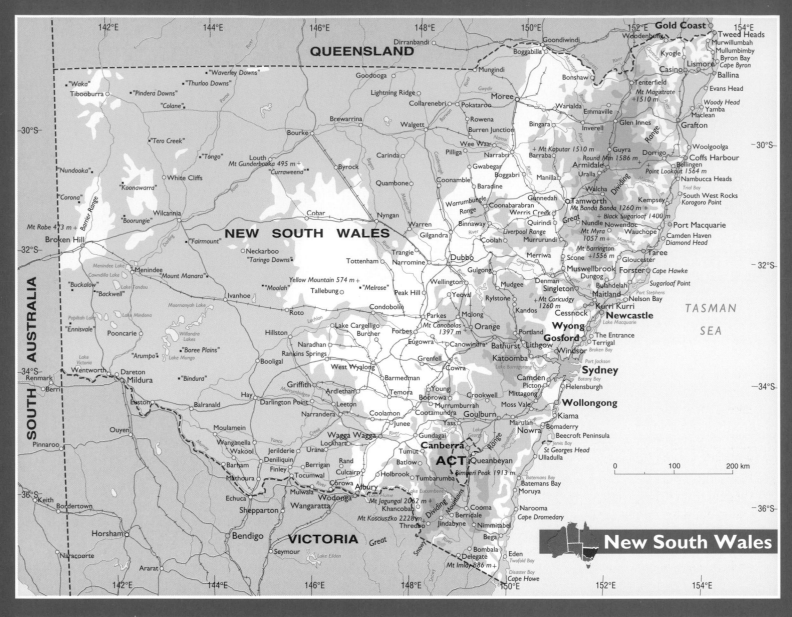

The Three Sisters in the Blue Mountains, west of Sydney.

New South Wales was the first Australian State established. Sydney, its capital city, is universally identified by its landmarks of Harbour, Bridge and Opera House. Besides being full of historic places, this great city has friendly people, some of the best restaurants anywhere, world-class entertainment and shopping, and magnificent green areas, both in the city heart and around the Harbour foreshore.

West from Sydney are the scenic splendours of the Blue Mountains. To the city's north is a coastal wonderland of lakes, beaches and resorts. Southwards are more beaches, magnificent coastal scenery and great fishing and seafood. The Great Dividing Range, from the Australian Alps north to the Border Ranges and Mt Warning, offers endless possibilities for adventures ranging from skiing and bushwalking to climbing, caving and whitewater rafting. More relaxing days can be spent exploring national parks, historic towns and gardens. Beyond the Great Divide are pastures, farmlands, scenic aridlands and mining communities, and the outback.

NEW SOUTH WALES

PAGES 10–29

SYDNEY & SURROUNDS

The Monorail travels above busy Sydney streets.

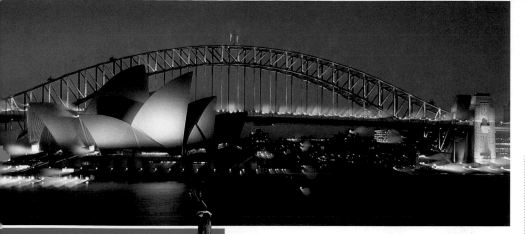

Sydney, the capital of the State of New South Wales, is Australia's largest city. Vibrant and vigorous, this harbourside city is multicultural yet uniquely Australian. Sydney's wonderful climate makes outdoor pastimes enjoyable the year round, while its galleries, theatres, shops and restaurants equal the world's best.

Viewing the harbour from a replica of Captain Bligh's *Bounty*.

SYDNEY'S EARLY HISTORY

Aboriginal people had lived in the area where Sydney now stands for tens of thousands of years when the British Royal Navy vessel *Endeavour* arrived in 1770. The ship's commander, Captain James Cook, RN, landed at Botany Bay and claimed eastern Australia for Britain.

In the 1780s England needed a place far from Europe to send convicts. Reports on the Botany Bay area by members of Cook's expedition led to the choice of New South Wales. Captain Arthur Phillip RN led the 11-ship First Fleet, which carried more than 1300 people (750 of them convicts) halfway around the world to found a settlement at Sydney Cove on 26 January 1788.

Free settlers soon arrived; farms were established and by 1810 the colony was home to more than 10 000 people. The crossing of the Blue Mountains in 1813 led to expansion over the Great Dividing Range to the rich grazing land beyond. The transportation of convicts continued until 1840.

BRIDGE AND OPERA HOUSE

The Harbour Bridge and Opera House (*above*) are international symbols of Sydney. Completed in 1932, the bridge spans 503 m and carries over 150 000 vehicles each day on a deck 59 m above sea level.

The Opera House, on Bennelong Point, cost $102 million to build. It was opened in 1973. Its tiled shell-roofs rise to 67 m above the harbour and cover nearly 2 ha. The largest theatre, the Concert Hall, seats 2690.

A Sydney ferry about to dock at Circular Quay.

SOME WAYS TO SEE SYDNEY

Discovering Sydney city on foot can be fun. Explorers can also use CityRail trains, or buses including the Sydney Explorer, which pauses at many attractions. An aerial train, the Monorail, loops between city centre, Darling Harbour and Chinatown. Ferries depart from Circular Quay to most harbour and Parramatta River destinations and a fast JetCat travels to and from Manly. A water taxi, hailed like a cab or called by phone, is a wonderful way to see the sights of the harbour.

A view of Sydney city over the Harbour as evening falls.

TEMP °C	J	F	M	A	M	J	J	A	S	O	N	D
MAX	26	26	25	22	19	17	16	18	20	22	24	25
MIN	19	19	17	15	11	9	8	9	11	13	16	17

Population: Nearly 4 million (55% of the population of NSW)
Rainfall: All months of the year, but most falls from January to July.

WHERE IS IT?

1	Farm Cove	10	Circular Quay
2	Kirribilli	11	Hyde Park
3	Kings Cross	12	Sydney Harbour Bridge
4	Opera House	13	Cahill Expressway
5	Royal Botanic Gardens	14	Sydney Tower
6	Government House	15	The Rocks
7	Woolloomooloo	16	Dawes Point Park
8	Bradfield Highway	17	Botany Bay
9	The Domain		

Sydney's oldest house, Cadman's Cottage, built in 1816.

The Garrison Church has stood in The Rocks since 1848.

SYDNEY'S PARKS AND GARDENS

Established in 1816 on the site of the colony's first farm on the shores of Farm Cove, Sydney's Royal Botanic Gardens is a haven of green tranquillity. It contains a fine Herbarium, a Tropical Centre, and palm, herb and other gardens. Included in its lush 30 ha is the Domain, a grassed area popular for concerts, picnics and outdoor speakers.

Hyde Park, even closer to the city's centre, was used from 1810 as a sports field and then a racecourse. Shady walks, the Anzac Memorial, the Archibald Fountain and a giant chessboard near the landmark of Busby's Bore Fountain can be found there.

THE HISTORIC ROCKS

The rocky area on the western side of Sydney Cove became the centre of Sydney Town soon after first settlement. Convicts hacked roadways from the sandstone; warehouses, hotels and dwellings were built; and The Rocks soon became a tough waterfront area. Today, restoration has re-created the atmosphere of old Sydney Town in The Rocks. Old pubs, historic buildings, a fine Museum of Contemporary Arts, an Observatory, and cafés, restaurants, shops and sightseeing await discovery. At weekends, The Rocks Market offers all sorts of art and craftwork.

TOWER AND MONORAIL

For a bird's-eye view of Sydney, take a lift to the Observation Level of the Sydney Tower, whose golden turret (*left*) also contains two revolving restaurants and a coffee shop. Nearly 300 m below, the regular grid of streets is studded with attractions such as the Queen Victoria Building. Further away can be found the Harbour, Botany Bay, the South Pacific Ocean and, to the west, the Blue Mountains. Allowing a more intimate view of the city, the Monorail (*left*) whisks around its circuit in 12 minutes, trains running at five-minute intervals and stopping at each of seven stations.

The Anzac Memorial and Pool of Remembrance in Hyde Park. The Memorial includes a military exhibition.

NEW SOUTH WALES

SHOPPING IN SYDNEY

The imposing statue (*left*) seated in regal splendour outside the Town Hall entrance to the Queen Victoria Building was rescued from Ireland. The QVB itself was once a disused produce market, which was refurbished to open in 1986 as a sumptuous shopping venue, whose four levels showcase nearly 200 magnificent shops and boutiques (*top*).

Pitt Street Mall's Strand Arcade has been a fashionable place to shop since 1892. Centrepoint (beneath the Sydney Tower), the Mid City Centre, Skygarden and the Harbourside Festival Marketplace at Darling Harbour are only a few of the city's many other great places to buy, browse and enjoy a day out.

The Dixon Street entrance to Sydney's Chinatown.

MUSEUMS AND GALLERIES

A cultural tour of Sydney is richly rewarding. The Art Gallery of New South Wales (*right*), whose highlights include the stunning Aboriginal and Torres Strait Islander Yiribani Gallery, leads the long list of places to see fine art. The city also offers many museums, notably the Australian Museum, rich in natural history, and the wonderful Powerhouse Museum, with its great interactive displays.

Sydney is crammed with places to eat, offering many cuisines.

EATING OUT IN SYDNEY

Whatever cuisine takes the diner's fancy can be found somewhere in Sydney, and some restaurants offer menus blending several ethnic styles. Seafood (*left*) is a specialty (Sydney Fish Markets are worth visiting). Diners have a wide choice of places to eat: The Rocks, Chinatown, Circular Quay, Paddington, Glebe, Darlinghurst; in fact, there are wonderful restaurants and cafés in most suburbs.

THEATRES AND ENTERTAINMENTS

From grand opera and symphony concerts to nightclubs and avant garde theatre, Sydney has entertainment to suit everyone. The Opera House is home to all sorts of events besides opera. The Sydney Entertainment Centre, the State Theatre, the Capitol and the Theatre Royal stage the big shows, while rock concerts may take over the Sydney Cricket Ground. There are plenty of smaller theatres as well.

The Sydney Festival, a month of cultural happenings and popular entertainment, climaxes in the Australia Day celebrations on 26 January and includes Opera in the Park, which is held in the Domain. The excitement the Festival generates continues for many in February's Mardi Gras and associated events. The Sydney Film Festival occupies two weeks in mid-June.

Sydney has plenty of nightclubs and bars. The pubs and clubs of Kings Cross and Woolloomooloo are internationally famous for their uninhibited entertainments.

George Street is home to cinemas and the Metro Theatre.

A feature of Kings Cross, the El Alamein Fountain.

A MAGNIFICENT HARBOUR

Sydney's fabulous harbour covers around 54 sq km, with a shoreline of about 300 km. "The finest harbour in the world," as Captain Phillip described it in 1788, is Sydney's playground – a place to swim, dive, fish, sail, powerboat or just admire the view. It has three main sections, North Harbour, Middle Harbour and Port Jackson, the area nearest to the Harbour Bridge. Its five islands include Fort Denison, once a prison known as Pinchgut. One of the most dramatic sights of Sydney's summer is the start of the Sydney to Hobart Yacht Race on 26 December.

RESERVES AND NATIONAL PARKS

The Sydney area contains a wealth of bushland, much of it protected in Sydney Harbour National Park. The many reserved areas on the harbour foreshore are home to abundant native wildlife. At the entrance to the harbour, South Head and North Head offer panoramic views of harbour and ocean, and there are walking tracks through the heathland. The fortifications at Middle Head date from the 19th century.

The first national park in Australia (1879), Royal National Park, lies to the south of Sydney; Ku-ring-gai Chase National Park is to the north.

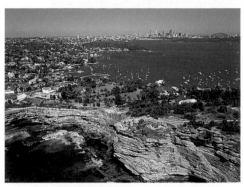

The cliffs of The Gap and the bulk of South Head bar the ocean from the protected waters of the harbour.

North Head Reserve is a haven for native birds.

DARLING HARBOUR

1. Cockle Bay
2. Convention and Exhibition Centre
3. Harbourside Festival Marketplace
4. National Maritime Museum
5. Pyrmont Bridge
6. Sydney Aquarium

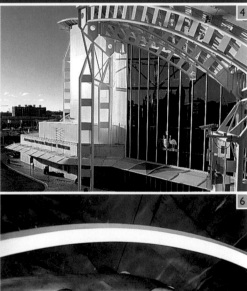

Originally named Cockle Bay, Darling Harbour was the site of Sydney's first steam mill, then an industrial suburb which became a waterside wasteland. Four years of intensive work saw the emergence of a splendid new city attraction, which opened in 1988. There is something happening every day of the year at Darling Harbour, from concerts to dragon boat racing, the International Boat Show or new attractions at the Maritime Museum or Sydney Aquarium.

NEW SOUTH WALES

IN THE OPEN AIR

Even in Sydney's most densely populated suburbs it is not far to a local park, and some very impressive open spaces are within a short bus ride of the city centre.

In the picture above, the famous Sydney Cricket Ground, battleground for national and international cricket and football matches, and the Sydney Football Stadium appear at centre left. Nearby are the extensive green spaces of Moore Park Golf Course and the park's many other excellent sporting facilities.

Adjoining the cricket ground is the Showground, now a film studio complex. (The new home of Sydney's Royal Easter Show is at Homebush Bay, site of the 2000 Olympics.) Beyond is Centennial Park, once a common where sheep and cows grazed. Now the park is 220 ha of lawns, lakes, ponds and gardens. There are trails for horse-riding and tracks for cycling, a café, and a sports ground.

South of Centennial Park is noted Randwick Racecourse, and several superb golf courses.

TARONGA ZOO

Taronga has surely the best position of any city zoo anywhere, right opposite Sydney city centre, easily accessible by ferry across the harbour or by bus across the Bridge. This marvellous zoo places emphasis on moats, rather than bars, to keep visitors and animals apart, and provides special viewing facilities for elusive animals such as the Koala (*far left above*), which can be observed from treetop level. Taronga breeds rare and endangered animals and specialises in Australian fauna.

The Elephant Temple (*left*) was completed for the opening of the zoo in 1916.

Paddington Bazaar, a place to shop and meet each Saturday.

MARKETS AND MEETING PLACES

Weekend markets have become a feature of Sydney. Bustling and busy, they are splendid place to buy and sell, to walk about, eat and drink, see people and be seen. Paddington Bazaar, held every Saturday, is the place for trendsetting fashion. Paddy's Market, held every weekend near Chinatown, is Sydney's oldest and features 800 stalls selling everything imaginable. There are markets also in Balmain and Glebe (each Saturday), at Bondi and on the boardwalk near the Opera House (each Sunday) and in The Rocks, on both Saturday and Sunday.

ARCHITECTURE ON DISPLAY

A stroll along Macquarie Street, which borders the western side of the Royal Botanic Gardens, will bring into view some of Sydney's most elegant buildings, including the Library of New South Wales, Parliament House and Sydney Hospital. The convict architect Francis Greenway designed the Hyde Park Barracks and St James' Church.

Juniper Hall in Paddington, Elizabeth Bay House in Elizabeth Bay and Vaucluse House in Vaucluse are wonderful reminders of the way in which rich folk lived in the nineteenth century. Further down the social scale were the workers of the Victorian and Edwardian eras. They lived with their sometimes large families in terrace houses in the inner suburbs. In time, these suburbs became shabby, but of recent years they have taken on new life and today terrace houses, many beautifully renovated, are in great demand.

Vaucluse House was begun in 1803. It was the home of explorer and politician W.C. Wentworth from 1829 to 1853.

SYDNEY'S FABULOUS BEACHES

Sydney Harbour offers many sandy beaches, which are safe and ideal for swimming. Some of the best-known southern harbour beaches are Watsons Bay (also noted for Doyles outdoor seafood restaurants), Shark Beach, Camp Cove and, for the adventurous, Lady Bay where nude bathing is permitted. On the north side of the harbour are Balmoral, Clontarf, Reef Beach and, most famous of all, Manly Cove, reached by ferry or JetCat. After a scenic harbour trip, a swim, a visit to Oceanworld and a meal at Manly Wharf can be followed by a pleasant stroll across the pedestrian mall known as The Corso to discover the Tasman Sea, part of the South Pacific Ocean, at Manly Beach, or at nearby Shelly or Fairy Bower Beaches.

Sydney's ocean beaches are world famous, and with good reason. Those north of Manly are often far less crowded than their counterparts south of the harbour entrance. Many are near parkland which contains enjoyable tracks and trails, and most are very scenic. Beaches such as Freshwater, Curl Curl, Dee Why and Narrabeen are popular with families and surfers and attract large crowds to Surf Lifesaving Carnivals.

The most famous ocean beach south of South Head is Bondi (*left*), a broad crescent of golden sand with terrific surf. As well as sun, surf and sand, Bondi offers restaurants and coffee shops. Further south are, among others, Tamarama, Bronte, Coogee, and the good surf beaches of Maroubra and Cronulla. All are within easy reach of the city by private or public transport.

Manly Ocean Beach with its rolling surf. Beyond is the sheltered harbour beach of Manly Cove.

SURF LIFESAVING

The Surf Lifesaving Association of Australia was formed in 1907. The lifesavers used wooden surf boats which are still seen in competition (*below*) but have been replaced by motorised rubber dinghies for everyday rescues. The surf reel (*right*), which anchors a lifesaver racing out to rescue a distressed swimmer, was invented at Bondi. Surf lifesaving carnivals are popular summer events. There are still plenty of bronzed male lifesavers, but the number of women (*left*) is increasing.

THE BLUE MOUNTAINS

The Three Sisters, and (*inset below*) a Crimson Rosella.

The haze that veils the Blue Mountains at a distance is caused by light striking tiny droplets of oil breathed out by the leaves of the eucalypt trees that clothe their sandstone. Part of the Great Dividing Range, the mountains rise about 65 km west of Sydney; for many years city-dwellers have taken refuge here from summer's heat. Today's visitors enjoy spectacular views, great bushwalking opportunities, abundant wildlife and some of Australia's loveliest gardens, featuring exotic and Australian native plants.

A BEAUTIFUL BARRIER

For 25 years, the sandstone cliffs of the Blue Mountains blocked European exploration to the west of Sydney. In 1813, three young colonials, Blaxland, Lawson and Wentworth, managed to cross the barrier by travelling along ridges rather than up valleys, which always ended in rock-faces. By 1815, convict labour had built a road across the mountains. Gold was discovered near Bathurst, to the west of the mountains, in the 1850s, and the railway had crossed the range by 1869. Luxurious hotels and fine residences, surrounded by lovely gardens, were built as mountain towns such as Katoomba became renowned as refuges from the city's summer heat and marvellous places to enjoy a holiday.

THE LEGEND OF THE THREE SISTERS

Some people say that once in the Blue Mountains there lived a clever old man, Tyawan. His three daughters were in danger from the powerful spirit Bunyip so, with his magic shinbone, Tyawan changed them into stone. To escape the Bunyip, he changed himself into a lyrebird, dropping the magic shinbone as he did so. Today, Tyawan, the lyrebird, still scratches through the leaves, trying to find his magic bone. Until he does so, he will remain a lyrebird, and his three lovely daughters will remain the stony Three Sisters.

The Katoomba Scenic Skyway soars past the Three Sisters.

The town of Katoomba looks out onto magnificent views.

THRILLS ON RAILS

At Katoomba, coal was once mined from a narrow seam below the cliffs. On the steep track up which coal trucks were once winched, the Scenic Railway (*left*) now carries entranced passengers swooping down to walking tracks below. The Zig-Zag Railway Line (*right*) was constructed between 1866 and 1869 to conquer rugged Mt Victoria. Bypassed in 1910, the line was re-opened in 1974 by steam-train enthusiasts and offers a nostalgic taste of a bygone era.

Above left: The thrills of the Scenic Railway.

Above: A treat for steam train buffs – the Zig Zag Railway.

HIGHLIGHTS OF THE BLUE MOUNTAINS

In the late nineteenth century, Sydney's citizens built cottages and mansions on large blocks of land in the Blue Mountains. From the 1880s, fine hotels rose at Katoomba, Medlow Bath, Jenolan Caves and Mt Victoria. Lovely formal gardens of flowering plants from the northern hemisphere were laid out, particularly at Katoomba, Blackheath and Leura. Today, magnificent avenues of deciduous trees and beds of glorious blooms make the Blue Mountains a mecca for garden-lovers, who can enjoy the many private gardens open to the public as well as public parks and gardens.

The highest town in the mountains, Blackheath, holds a rhododendron festival each November. Mount Tomah Botanic Gardens, a major attraction, is home to the impressive sundial shown below, and is noted for colourful deciduous trees, on show during autumn. Leura's Spring Festival is held in mid-October.

Those interested in art should not miss the Norman Lindsay Museum and Art Gallery at Faulconbridge.

There are many sights concentrated in the area which includes Katoomba and the Jamison Valley. Echo Point, on the rim of the valley, offers a view of the Three Sisters, the Ruined Castle and Mount Solitary. Wentworth Falls, a superb double waterfall, tumbles into this valley. Nearby, the Leura Cascades are floodlit at night.

To the north is the Grose Valley, whose grandeur is best seen from Govetts Leap.

Wentworth Falls, named after the explorer and politician.

Beauchamp Falls, Blue Mountains National Park.

Mt Wilson is noted for its wonderful gardens, at their most beautiful in spring and autumn.

The Waratah (*above*) and the Crimson Rosella (*opposite page*) are familiar sights in the Blue Mountains. They are only two of the myriads of spectacular native plants and animals of the region.

THE JENOLAN CAVES

The spectacular Jenolan Caves have been carved out of the limestone of the western edge of the Blue Mountains by the rushing Jenolan River. There are at least 300 caverns, each of them full of stony formations ranging in shape from grandly grotesque to delicately lovely. Electric lighting illuminates many of the more impressive caves and many visitors enjoy guided underground tours. Other mountainside features, such as Carlotta's Arch, the Devil's Coachhouse and Grand Arch may be explored at any time.

NATIONAL PARKS OF THE MOUNTAINS

The golden sandstone cliffs typical of the Blue Mountains may be 200 m high. Waterfalls drop from high valleys over these cliffs, into ravines in which grow rainforests which are relics of primeval times and which contain a wealth of wildlife. Many of the wild places of the Blue Mountains are protected by the Blue Mountains National Park, whose walking tracks take nature-lovers into an enchanted world of waterfalls, lookouts and forested valleys resounding to the lyrebird's call. On the mountains' western aspect, Kanangra Boyd National Park contains dramatic wilderness.

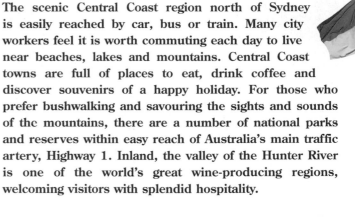

Surf fishing on a Central Coast beach. and (inset) a Silver Gull.

The scenic Central Coast region north of Sydney is easily reached by car, bus or train. Many city workers feel it is worth commuting each day to live near beaches, lakes and mountains. Central Coast towns are full of places to eat, drink coffee and discover souvenirs of a happy holiday. For those who prefer bushwalking and savouring the sights and sounds of the mountains, there are a number of national parks and reserves within easy reach of Australia's main traffic artery, Highway 1. Inland, the valley of the Hunter River is one of the world's great wine-producing regions, welcoming visitors with splendid hospitality.

GREEN PLACES NORTH OF SYDNEY

Once, the rich shoreline and lakes of the Central Coast provided abundant fish, shellfish and other food for the Awabakal and Darkinjang Aboriginal people. After Europeans arrived, the abundant forests which grew on the hill slopes were logged and boat-building became a local industry.

Some of the wild places have been preserved in national parks. Travellers heading north from Sydney pass through the rugged sandstones of Ku-ring-gai Chase National Park. Brisbane Water National Park lies south and west of Gosford, curling around Brisbane Water and the Hawkesbury River.

Bouddi National Park covers the north of the entrance to Broken Bay, while Dharug National Park, with its majestic sandstone escarpments, is on the western side of the Central Coast.

A REGION OF BEACHES AND LAKES

The Central Coast is rich in sandy ocean beaches, bordering the South Pacific Ocean. Behind these beaches is a chain of lakes and waterways, around which have been established farms, towns and resorts. Holiday-makers flock to the area, but there is plenty of room for all to share the Central Coast's peace and natural beauty.

Another glorious day at a typical Central Coast beach.

A view over Gosford to Brisbane Water National Park.

SOME CENTRAL COAST TOWNS

Gosford is the first major town on the highway to Sydney's north, and is sited close to Brisbane Water National Park, with its Aboriginal engravings and unspoiled beaches. Two other attractions of Gosford are the Australian Reptile Park and the historical re-enactments at Old Sydney Town. The nearby resorts of Killcare, McMasters Beach and Avoca Beach are popular with holiday-makers. East of Gosford is Terrigal, where a spectacular bluff known as The Skillion protects a fine beach and a safe boat harbour.

Brisbane Water National Park.

Fun in the sun on Avoca Beach.

Terrigal is a popular resort within easy reach of Sydney.

A vista in Wollemi National Park.

The Entrance guards the opening to the wonderland that is Tuggerah Lakes. (*Inset*) Australian Pelican.

WILD PLACES OF THE GREAT DIVIDE

Some of Australia's grandest wild country lies in the Great Divide inland from the Central Coast. Wollemi National Park, between the Blue Mountains and the Hunter Valley, is the largest forested wilderness remaining in NSW and harbours unique plants, including the Wollemi Pine, a relic of the rainforests which covered Australia many millions of years ago. Yengo National Park shares the Wollemi's landscape of sheer cliffs, deep gorges and sparkling, rushing rivers. To the north, Barrington Tops National Park is World Heritage listed for its diversity of plant life.

LAKELAND PLAYGROUNDS

North of Brisbane Water are Tuggerah Lakes, three adjoining waterways whose connection to the ocean is guarded by the town of The Entrance. The Australian Pelicans common along this coastline are particularly tame here. To the north of Tuggerah Lakes lies Lake Macquarie, four times the size of Sydney Harbour and the playground for Newcastle city. It has over 250 km of foreshore, and provides plenty of places to fish, boat and picnic. Myall Lakes, north of Newcastle, are brackish bodies of water, barred from the sea by sand dunes. Myall Lakes National Park protects dunes, waterways and surrounding bushlands.

Queen's Wharf, a Newcastle waterfront landmark.

NEWCASTLE — A WELCOMING CITY

Coal was discovered at Newcastle in 1791 and was being exported to Bengal by 1799. Despite evidence of its industrial history, this city at the mouth of the Hunter River is near to excellent beaches and the joys of Lake Macquarie. With its multicultural population, Newcastle is noted for great food, fine wines (remember the Hunter Valley is nearby) and warm hospitality. It also offers many classic Victorian buildings which survived the earthquake of 1989. The restored Queen's Wharf is a waterfront feature, and Fort Scratchley houses a Maritime Museum. (Built in fear of a Russian invasion in the 1880s, the fort eventually fired its guns when a Japanese submarine entered the harbour in 1942.)

THE HUNTER VALLEY

The Convent at Pepper Tree is guest house for a winery.

The Hunter Valley, where some of Australia's great table wines are produced, is only two hours' drive from Sydney. Vines have been grown here since the 1830s, and the Upper and Lower Hunter Valley boast more than 70 wineries. Towns such as Maitland and Cessnock have many historic buildings and are famous for their restaurants. They make good bases from which to visit the wineries to sample and purchase their wares. Hot air ballooning and golf are pleasant alternatives to wine-tasting.

Cessnock School of Arts.

Northern coastal New South Wales enjoys a subtropical climate, and is one of Australia's great holiday destinations. The coastline's towns offer relaxed lifestyles, superb seafood, sailing and surfing. The hinterland, with its rugged ranges and whitewater rivers such as the Nymboida, has many places of unspoiled beauty. Over the Great Dividing Range lies New England Tableland, a variety of gemfields and some fascinating national parks.

Perfect swells at Wategos, Byron Bay.

Crowdy Head in Crowdy Bay National Park, near Port Macquarie.

BYRON BAY

Cape Byron is the most easterly point on the Australian mainland. It rises 100 m above the ocean and and is crowned by a lighthouse (*left*) whose powerful beam is visible 40 km out to sea.

For many years, timber felled on the slopes of the ranges behind Byron Bay skidded down steep gullies called "shoots" then was hauled to the sea and loaded on to freighters. Later the area became known for dairying. Today, Byron Bay is a stylish seaside town, with great surfing at Wategos and other beaches, fishing, whale-watching, and hang-gliders (*right*) which soar far above the cape and its lighthouse.

Fishing vessels like these in Coffs Harbour supply the superb fresh seafood for which this coast is famous.

PORT MACQUARIE AND "COFFS"

Port Macquarie, on the mouth of the Hastings River, was once a penal settlement and is now a busy fishing port. Coffs Harbour, originally a timber port, is today home to a modern fishing fleet and a wide variety of pleasure craft. Nearby Muttonbird Island is the breeding ground for thousands of seabirds.

A secluded beach at Port Macquarie.

Cape Byron lighthouse stands on Australia's most easterly point.

Sand, surf and sunshine, hallmarks of the north coast, NSW.

WORLD HERITAGE WILDERNESS

In the Great Dividing Range west of Coffs Harbour are several fine wilderness areas protected by national parks. The World Heritage listed Dorrigo National Park includes temperate rainforests rich in plants and wildlife, and scenic treasures such as Crystal Shower Falls (*right*), a short distance from the excellent Visitors' Centre and canopy-viewing Skywalk. Nearby New England National Park is also a World Heritage listed area, where visitors can experience subalpine forest as well as temperate and subtropical rainforests.

RAINFOREST, THE GREEN TREASURE

There are several different sorts of rainforest in Australia. Although they are found in different climatic regions or at different altitudes, they all require a regular, steady supply of rain. In the past 200 years, much of the easily accessible temperate and subtropical rainforests of New South Wales have been logged, or cleared for farming. The areas remaining are recognised as remarkable natural treasures, home to unique plants and to mammals, birds and other creatures found nowhere else.

Ebor Falls in Guy Fawkes River National Park.

NEW ENGLAND TABLELAND

The university city of Armidale is the major centre of the beautiful New England Tableland, a highlands area famed for excellent livestock (*below*), magnificent displays of autumn leaves, some of the State's most picturesque national parks and Bald Rock, a huge granite monolith near the town of Tenterfield. The Fossickers' Way takes would-be gem hunters from Tamworth through Inverell to Glen Innes, in search of sapphires and other stones.

New England National Park is known for diversity.

Mount Warning is the core of an ancient volcano.

BORN IN FIRE

Millions of years ago, a chain of volcanoes 800 km in length existed in eastern Australia. Today, Mt Warning, in the extreme north-east of NSW, Mt Kaputar, near Narrabri, and the Warrumbungle Range, on the western edge of the Great Divide near Coonabarabran, are the weathered cores of extinct mountains of fire. Warrumbungle National Park is noted for its spectacular scenery. This is where the plants and animals of the well-watered east coast blend with those of the drier western plains and inland deserts, and springtime in the Warrumbungles is rich with wildflowers and nesting birds.

Wedge-tailed Eagle

The Breadknife, at right, in the Warrumbungles was formed from molten rock forced into a crack, cooled, then exposed.

On the western side of the Great Divide, annual rainfall decreases dramatically. Towns and farms draw water from the network of creeks and rivers that drain into the Murrumbidgee and the Darling and, eventually, the mighty Murray. Stock and wildlife drink at bores drawing water from the ancient reservoirs of the Great Artesian Basin. When heavy rain does fall, the dry plains of the far west are transformed. This is the time to see the desert in bloom.

Sheep graze on the plains west of the Great Dividing Range.

HEADING WEST

West of the Great Dividing Range lies some of Australia's best pastoral and agricultural country. The road stretches through fields of wheat or other crops, or between paddocks where cattle or sheep graze contentedly. The line of a creek is marked by eucalypt trees, in whose sheltering branches cockatoos such as the Major Mitchell (*above*) shelter from the heat of the day. Country towns, each with its distinguishing features (the church, *inset right*, is in Nevertire, on the Mitchell Highway north-west of Dubbo) pass by. As the countryside grows steadily drier, fences become less frequent, bush takes over from cultivation and the true outback surrounds the traveller. This is the place to stop the car, get out, and listen to the sounds of Australia.

The Western Plains Zoo has successfully bred the Cheetah.

A ZOO ON THE WESTERN PLAINS

Western Plains Zoo, near Dubbo, is the "free-range" offspring of Sydney's Taronga Zoo. At the Plains Zoo, the natural bushland has been divided by waterways, which form boundaries for animal groups, and roads to provide access for visitors. A wonderful day can be spent at the zoo, watching lion, rhinoceros, zebra, giraffe, and a wide variety of other animals roaming in spacious areas landscaped to resemble their natural habitats.

THE RICHES OF THE EARTH

Minerals have made a great contribution to the prosperity of central and western New South Wales and helped establish communities in some of the State's most remote areas. Often more than one mineral is present in an area: Cobar, in the north-west, produces copper, zinc, silver, lead and gold. Broken Hill, in the south-west, produces silver, lead and zinc.

Fossickers can spend days searching for precious gems such as sapphires in the New England area, or head to Lightning Ridge near the Queensland border, or go westwards to White Cliffs in the quest for opals (*left*). Lightning Ridge is the black opal capital of the world, and visitors to the town are allowed to investigate surface heaps of mullock (clay discarded from the mines) in hopes of finding specks of colour or even a sizeable piece of iridescent gemstone.

These eucalypts and wattles flourish in arid country.

The Court House at Cobar, a copper-mining town.

Silverton, near Broken Hill, was once a silver boom town and is now a centre for art and a film location.

The Living Desert sculptures stand near Broken Hill.

MINING AND CULTURE

The rich silver, lead and zinc ore discovered near Broken Hill and Silverton, in far south-western NSW, in the 1870s and 80s led to important mining ventures. Broken Hill is still one of the world's great mining towns and boasts some fine National-Trust-classified historic buildings. It is also famous for its many galleries. Silverton is a ghost town, which is also a home for artists, and an ideal location for film and TV crews making features about the outback.

The Darling River system drains vast areas as it flows from Queensland to where it joins the Murray River at Wentworth, NSW. Here it is seen in Kinchega National Park, south-east of Broken Hill.

Modern sculpture and turn-of-the-century Trades Hall symbolise Broken Hill's blend of mining and art.

ARID-COUNTRY RESERVES

Mungo National Park, in the south-western corner of NSW, was proclaimed a World Heritage site in 1981. Its sand dunes preserve fossil evidence of the way people lived beside the freshwater lakes which existed here some 40 000 years ago.

Willandra National Park, about 200 km north of Hay, and, like Mungo, not easy of access, was for years part of an enormous sheep station. Today it is notable for its wildlife and the scenic areas along Willandra Creek.

The half-moon dunes of Mungo National Park.

WESTERN WILDLIFE

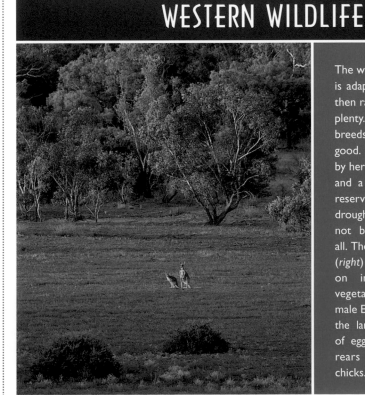

The wildlife of the western plains is adapted to a cycle of drought then rainfall and a brief period of plenty. The Red Kangaroo (*left*) breeds freely when times are good. A female may have a joey by her side, another in her pouch and a third, still an embryo, in reserve. In time of drought she will not breed at all. The Emu (*right*) feeds on insects and vegetation. The male Emu broods the large clutch of eggs, then rears the chicks.

A fishing trawler in dock at Batemans Bay.

THE SOUTHERN HIGHLANDS

The Southern Highlands is a tableland area which begins about 100 km south of Sydney. It rises to nearly 900 m above sea level, and its temperate climate, clearly defined seasons and fertile soil mean that towns such as Mittagong, Bowral, Berrima, Moss Vale and Bundanoon are noted for their parks and gardens. Each October, Bowral is home to the Tulip Time Festival. Bundanoon is known for its Glow Worm Glen. Nattai National Park and the fascinating Wombeyan Caves lie west of the highlands. To the east, the tableland drops away to the coastal plain down the Illawarra escarpment.

Kangaroo Valley typifies the beauty of this area — the whole valley is classified by the National Trust — and a Pioneer Museum displays relics of the valley's past. Visitors to the town of Kangaroo Valley are always fascinated by the gate-towers of Hampden Bridge (above), which has spanned the Kangaroo River since 1898.

Beautiful Kangaroo Valley.

South of Sydney, a chain of superb white surf beaches interrupted by scenic headlands stretches to the Victorian border. This is paradise for anyone who loves the sea, marine exploration, fishing or sailing. Happy days can be spent just relaxing in any one of the holiday towns to be found between mountains and ocean. Once, the forests that covered those mountains were logged for timber and the coastal plains were cleared for dairying. Today, national parks preserve scenic places in the ranges and along the coast.

A lighthouse was built on Wollongong's Flagstaff Point in 1872.

Kiama's famous blowhole is on rocky Blowhole Point.

WOLLONGONG AND BEYOND

Located 80 km south of Sydney, beyond Royal National Park, Wollongong is Australia's seventh-largest city, famous for coal and steel production. Today, industrial shipping docks in neighbouring Port Kembla, and Wollongong's historic harbour is a base for marine pleasure activities. Further south, the town of Kiama is famous for its blowhole,

which in high seas fountains water up to 60 m into the air. In nearby Budderoo National Park, the award-winning Minnamurra Rainforest Centre offers visitors a view of rainforest canopy from an elevated boardwalk.

Morton National Park is one of the largest national parks in New South Wales. It protects a rugged stretch of the Great Dividing Range where rivers such as the Shoalhaven have carved scenic gorges though the sandstone.

Belmore Falls, Morton National Park.

Carrington Falls, Budderoo National Park.

Eastern Grey Kangaroos welcome walkers near the beach at Murramarang National Park, just north of Batemans Bay.

SOUTHERN COASTAL TOWNS

Bodalla, Narooma, Bermagui, Tathra, Merimbula, Eden – the names of the major towns of the southern coast of New South Wales are a roll-call of wonderful places to holiday and relax. They are famous for their silver surf beaches and sparkling blue sea, and for the fresh-caught seafood to be sampled in every town. Visitors who wish to catch their own fish dinner can choose between wetting a line in the ocean or casting for trout in the swift-moving rivers flowing from the Great Divide.

The town of Bega, about 10 minutes inland from Tathra, is the unofficial capital of the area. It is renowned for its cheeses.

GREEN AND SCENIC PLACES

Between Ulladulla and Batemans Bay, the narrow coastal Murramarang National Park offers secluded beaches and plentiful wildlife. Kangaroos and wallabies are particularly easy to meet at Pebbly Beach. Further south, Wallagoot Lake is popular for fishing and boating, while the bordering Bournda National Park has plenty of walking trails and picnic spots.

North and south of Eden are the two sections of Ben Boyd National Park. The rock formation called the Pinnacles is a notable feature of the north, while in the south is Boyds Tower, built in the 1840s as a lighthouse but never used as such.

"Living village", Central Tilba, is National Trust classified.

Fishing and seafood are part of the south coast lifestyle.

JERVIS BAY

In 1915, Jervis Bay was transferred from NSW to the ACT to give Canberra access to the sea and a site for the Royal Australian Navy Training College. It is a superb area for fishing, boating and bushwalking and is noted for the diversity and richness of its underwater life. Point Perpendicular guards the bay entrance on the northern side.

At Tathra, Australian Pelicans wait for the fishing boats to return with their tasty catch.

Point Perpendicular.

A Humpback Whale breaches in a flurry of spray.

WHALES SWIM THESE WATERS

For many years, whaling was the chief occupation of the men of Eden, a port about 500 km south of Sydney. The story goes that a pack of Killer Whales worked with the human hunters herding other whales into Twofold Bay. Today Eden's Killer Whale Museum and Davidson Whaling Station Historic Site pay tribute to the whaling days. In October and November whale-watching vessels join the fishing fleet that uses magnificent Twofold Bay as a home port.

Perisher, one of the highest ski resorts in the Snowy Mts, caters for all ages.

The magnificent alpine country of south-eastern New South Wales was a well-kept secret for many years before the Snowy Mountains scheme constructed a system of roads, tunnels, dams and power stations to provide hydro-electric power and irrigation reservoirs. Suddenly access to the high country in both winter and summer became easy and the fame of Australia's Alps spread worldwide. Today Kosciuszko National Park stretches along the Great Divide from the ACT to the Victorian border. It contains Mt Kosciuszko, the highest mountain in Australia (2228 m), a group of excellent ski resorts and vast stretches of rugged wilderness rich in mountains, lakes and exceptional wildlife.

The sun shines through crystals of ice.

TOURING THE ALPS

The snow and ice that make winter in the Australian Alps such fun can also pose transportation problems for visitors to the snowfields. In winter months, anti-freeze compound should be used in vehicle radiators, and it is compulsory to carry wheel chains in certain sections of the Snowy Mountains between 1 June and 10 October each year.

Many visitors enjoy seeing the mountains from the Skitube train whose terminal is at Bullocks Flat. The train crosses the Crackenback Range, then climbs through stands of lofty Alpine Ash and magnificent Snow Gums before allowing enthralled passengers panoramic views of Thredbo Valley. After travelling underground, the train pauses at Perisher and Mount Blue Cow before returning to base. Skiing equipment (or, in summer, mountain bikes) can be hired at the Bullocks Flat terminal.

A snowman joins the fun in the Australian Alps.

RESORTS FOR SNOW SPORTS

Snow-sporters can choose from Thredbo (caters for skiers at all levels and has a year-round chairlift to the summit of Mt Crackenback), Charlotte Pass (a good base for tours to the higher peaks), Perisher (caters for both downhill and cross-country skiers) and Smiggin Holes (particularly good for not-so-experienced skiers). Skitube runs from Bullocks Flat Terminal via Perisher to Blue Cow Mountain.

The imposing snow covered slopes of the Australian Alps in winter.

SLEEPING WINTER AWAY

The high country has a rich and varied animal population. One of the most remarkable wild creatures is the Mountain Pygmy-possum. This tiny marsupial (an adult would fit comfortably in the palm of an adult person's hand) is found only where snow covers the ground for up to six months of the year. Before the first snowfall of the season, a possum eats seeds and insects greedily, doubling its body weight, then it sleeps away the winter in a snug nest. There are probably no more than 2600 Mountain Pygmy-possums in existence today, and the total area in which they are found is less than 10 sq km.

A hardy Snow Gum.

The Mountain Pygmy-possum spends winter under the snow.

An alpine stream subdued by winter's chill.

Spring blossom brings colour to the high country.

Lake Jindabyne in summer.

WHERE WOMBATS WANDER

Common Wombats are large, bulky animals (an adult weighs about 26 kg), and they find it difficult to move through snow. In summer they emerge from their woodland burrows in the late afternoon, then graze and find roots and fungi well into the night. During winter and early spring, they may be seen at any hour of the day feeding where plants have been exposed by shifting snow, often on the sides of roads, or making their way to lower altitudes to look for food. A young wombat is born in autumn. It remains safe in its mother's warm pouch until summer, when food can be easily found.

SUMMER'S HIGH DELIGHTS

Above an altitude of 1900 m in the Australian Alps, even the tough Snow Gums cannot get enough solar energy to sustain their growth. The higher slopes are covered by low heaths, which manage to survive under a blanket of snow for at least four months each year. When spring comes, the snow slowly thaws and all the mountain creeks begin to run with melt-water.

As the warmth of the sun and the length of the days increase, the heathlands become bright with flowers. The slopes of the mountains come alive with the murmur of running water, the sweet songs of birds and the happy sounds of bushwalkers, campers and anglers making the most of the spectacular scenery, the placid lakes and trout-filled streams while summer lasts.

LORD HOWE ISLAND

Lord Howe Island and nearby islets are administered from NSW and can be reached after a flight of about two hours from either Sydney or Brisbane. Temperate climate and abundant natural beauty combine to make these jewels of the South Pacific all-year-round holiday destinations.

Mt Gower (875 m) and Mt Lidgbird (765 m) dominate Lord Howe Island.

Balls Pyramid is 2 km south-east of Lord Howe Island.

Lord Howe, the Admiralty Islands and Balls Pyramid were first sighted by Lt Henry Lidgbird Ball in 1788 and were settled in the early 1840s. Today they are a paradise for holiday-makers, snorkellers and scuba-divers, walkers, climbers and nature lovers. The islands' coral reefs are home to around 500 sorts of fish, and birdwatchers can sight more than 120 species, including the Red-tailed Tropicbird (*right*).

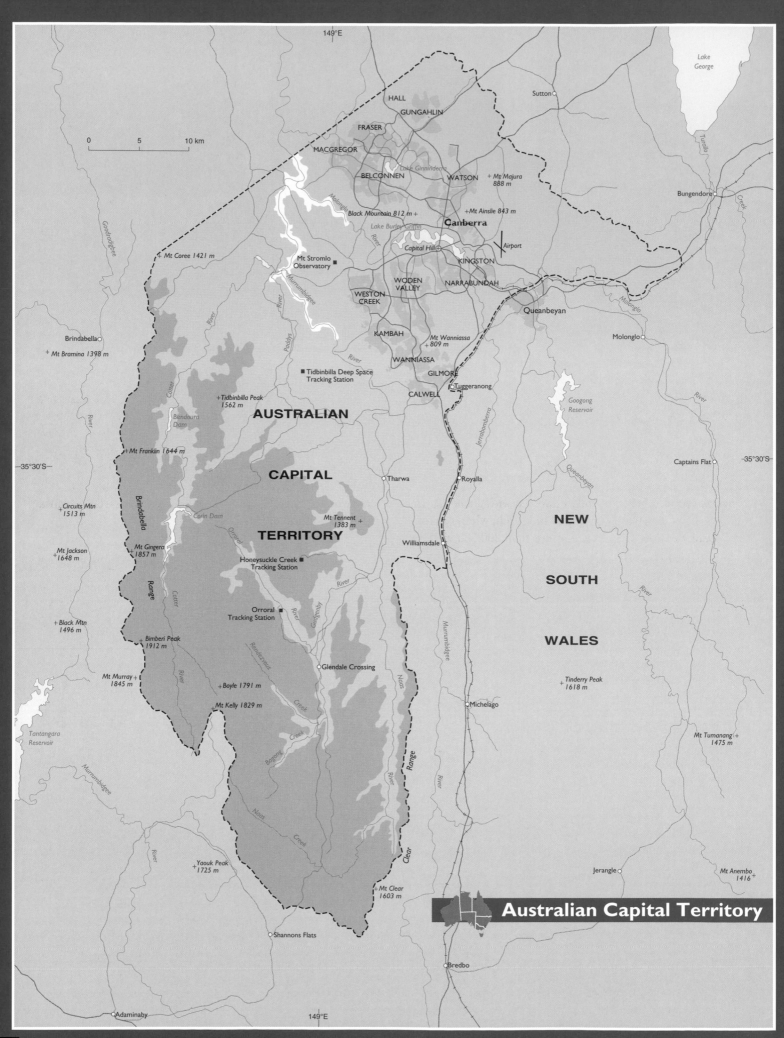

149°E

Lake
George

Turallo

0   5   10 km

HALL

GUNGAHLIN

Sutton

FRASER

MACGREGOR

BELCONNEN

Lake Ginninderra

WATSON

+ Mt Majura
888 m

Bungendore

Creek

Molonglo

Black Mountain 812 m +

+Mt Ainslie 843 m

Lake Burley Griffin

Canberra

River

+ Mt Coree 1421 m

Mt Stromlo
Observatory

Capital Hill +

Airport

Murrumbidgee

KINGSTON

WODEN
VALLEY

NARRABUNDAH

Goodradigbee

River

WESTON
CREEK

Queanbeyan

Molonglo

Brindabella

KAMBAH

Mt Wanniassa
+ 809 m

Molonglo

+ Mt Bramina 1398 m

Paddys

River

WANNIASSA

Tidbinbilla Deep Space
Tracking Station

GILMORE

Tuggeranong

Jerrabomberra

Googong
Reservoir

River

CALWELL

River

+Tidbinbilla Peak
1562 m

AUSTRALIAN

Bendoura
Dam

Cotter

Queanbeyan

Captains Flat

+Mt Franklin 1644 m

CAPITAL

Tharwa

Royalla

−35°30'S

River

Corin Dam

NEW

Circuits Mtn
+ 1513 m

Brindabella

Orroral

Mt Tennent
1383 m +

TERRITORY

SOUTH

Mt Jackson
+ 1648 m

Mt Gingera
+ 1857 m

Honeysuckle Creek
Tracking Station

River

Williamsdale

Range

Cotter

WALES

River

Murrumbidgee

+ Black Mtn
1496 m

Orroral
Tracking Station

River

Gudgenby

Tinderry Peak
+ 1618 m

+Bimberi Peak
1912 m

Glendale Crossing

Naas

Rendezvous

Mt Murray +
1845 m

River

+Boyle 1791 m

Tantangara
Reservoir

Creek

+Mt Kelly 1829 m

Range

Clear

Michelago

Mt Tumanang
+ 1475 m

Bogong

Murrumbidgee

Naas

River

Clear

Jerangle

Mt Anembo
1416 +

River

+Yaouk Peak
1725 m

Creek

+ Mt Clear
1603 m

Australian Capital Territory

Shannons Flats

Bredbo

Adaminaby

149°E

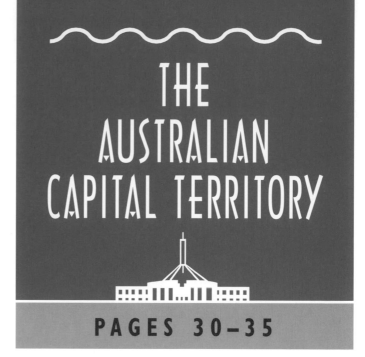

THE AUSTRALIAN CAPITAL TERRITORY

PAGES 30-35

Surrounded by NSW, the ACT is the setting for the nation's capital city, Canberra, in the beautiful valley of the Molonglo River which was dammed to form Lake Burley Griffin. Nearly half of the ACT is set aside for parks and reserves, including Namadgi National Park. The ACT offers the full gamut, from sophisticated city life to experiences of pristine bushland and fascinating wildlife.

About halfway between Sydney and Melbourne, Canberra is an easy few hours by road from either. Founded in 1913, it was designed to be the home of Australia's Federal institutions and diplomatic missions from abroad. Multicultural and hospitable, this lovely city is a place where people can explore Australia's past, present and future in a city planned to reflect the national spirit.

Spacious and magnificently endowed with gardens, the National Capital is at its very best in March, when the ten-day Canberra Festival attracts more than 200 000 visitors to celebrate its founding. Brilliant autumn leaves form a blazing backdrop to concerts, a street parade, an outdoor art exhibition and the fireworks of Skyfire. Trademarks of this birthday party are the multicoloured hot-air balloons that soar from the Parliamentary foreshore at dawn and carry their enthralled passengers buoyantly over the city.

The other great festival is in springtime, when Floriade fills Commonwealth Park with floral splendour and crowds enjoy the city's private and public gardens and a host of cultural events.

CANBERRA 32

CANBERRA & SURROUNDS

Commonwealth Park during Floriade.

Parliament House (*above*) and its steel flag mast (*above left*).

Australia's Federal Capital, Canberra is one of the world's very few planned cities. It has grown in orderly fashion, untouched by wars or natural catastrophes, and is laid out to make exploration easy. Canberra is a spacious and gracious city, whose visual appeal is enhanced by scenic Lake Burley Griffin. Its public buildings display Australia's treasures to the world and its parks and gardens are magnificent, particularly during springtime and when autumn turns deciduous leaves to bronze.

ON THE MOLONGLO

The area on which Canberra stands today, on the Limestone Plains crossed by the Molonglo River, was for tens of thousands of years the home of the Aboriginal Walgalu and Ngunawal people. In 1820, Charles Throsby and Joseph Wild were the first Europeans to see the area. Land grants were made by Governor Macquarie to settlers in 1821 and by 1825 graziers like Robert Campbell had established flocks there. The first recorded use of "Canberry", translated as "a meeting place", dates to 1826.

The Federation of the Australian States in 1901 brought intense rivalry between Sydney and Melbourne as to which should be the Federal Capital. The Australian Capital Territory, consisting of 2400 sq km situated about midway between Sydney and Melbourne, was transferred from NSW in 1910. The Commonwealth assumed control in 1911, and the city of Canberra was founded in 1913.

A PLANNED CITY

Today the population of Canberra is over 285 000, and its suburbs have spread over the Limestone Plains. Thanks to the brilliant vision of landscape architect Walter Burley Griffin, who planned Canberra to take advantage of the natural features of the Molonglo basin, its growth has been orderly. Locals and visitors manage to travel easily between centres of business, government and residence.

Walter Burley Griffin planned that Canberra city should focus upon a "land axis" aligned from Bimberi Peak to Mount Ainslie. A "water axis" formed by a lake would cross this. The buildings housing the great federal institutions would form a triangle whose base ran along the lake and whose apex was Parliament House, on Capital Hill. The full realisation of Burley Griffin's vision began in 1964 with the flooding of Lake Burley Griffin, and was complete when Parliament House was opened in 1988.

Blundell's Farmhouse, built for Robert Campbell's ploughman William Ginn in 1858 and later occupied by the Blundell family.

Duntroon House was built by Robert Campbell in 1833.

HISTORIC CANBERRA

There are many fascinating historical buildings to be seen in Canberra and its surrounds. Any tour should take in the legacy of Sydney merchant Robert Campbell, which includes Duntroon House, begun in the 1830s and extended in the 1860s, and Blundell's Farmhouse (1858). In Reid stands the church of St John the Baptist, consecrated in 1845. Many of the district's first settlers are buried in its graveyard. South of the city is the homestead "Lanyon", which was built in 1859 and houses a collection of Sidney Nolan paintings. At Watson, a Heritage Village displays how Australians lived 100 years ago.

Balloons on the shore of Lake Burley Griffin celebrate the Canberra Festival.

TEMP °C	J	F	M	A	M	J	J	A	S	O	N	D
MAX	28	27	24	20	15	12	11	13	16	19	23	26
MIN	13	13	11	7	3	1	0	1	3	6	9	11

WHERE IS IT?

1 Lake Burley Griffin	10 National Library
2 Various embassies	11 Questacon
3 National University	12 Old Parlt House
4 Civic (city centre)	13 Mount Ainslie
5 City Hill	14 War Memorial
6 Capital Hill	15 Anzac Parade
7 Parliament House	16 High Court
8 Capt Cook Water Jet	17 National Gallery
9 Commonwealth Pk	18 Carillon

Entrance to Parliament House is through the pillars of the Great Verandah.

The Forecourt of Parliament House features a mosaic, based on artwork by Aboriginal artist Michael Tjakamarra Nelson, showing a symbolic meeting place.

The House of Representatives Chamber.

The Senate Chamber.

PARLIAMENT HOUSE

The magnificent building that was opened by Her Majesty Queen Elizabeth II on 9 May 1988 reflects the commitment of the Australian people to parliamentary democracy. The people's elected representatives meet here, in a complex open to visitors on 364 days of every year.

Public entrance is through the imposing pillars of the Great Verandah, into the majestic Foyer (*inset above*), whose 48 grey-green, marble-clad pillars evoke the trunks of stately eucalypt trees. Beyond the Foyer are the Great Hall and the Members Hall, flanked by the House of Representatives and Senate Chambers.

The present Parliament House that stands on Capital Hill replaced a provisional building sited nearer the lake. It was constructed in 1927 and today is a conference centre. Of the newer building, much is below the surface of Capital Hill, and the visible elements – including massive but graceful wings shaped like boomerangs, a grassed walkway and a flagpole 81 m high – do not impede the view from Bimberi Peak to Mount Ainslie.

The treasures that may be seen within Parliament House include the Parliament House Art Collection, an Historic Memorials Collection and a Gift Collection.

The Captain Cook Terrestrial Globe on Regatta Point.

Autumn leaves blaze red and gold in Canberra gardens.

FLORIADE

From mid-September to mid-October each year, Canberra is on show as it celebrates Floriade, the Federal Capital's annual festival of flowers. Half-a-million enchanted visitors wander through Canberra's Commonwealth Park, admiring the glorious displays of tulips (*above and inset below*), daffodils, hyacinths and other bulbs. Since 1988, Floriade has become one of Canberra's two great festivals (the other is the Canberra Festival held in mid-March).

Floriade is much more than just a garden display. It incorporates a wide range of cultural events and many of the city's most beautiful private gardens are opened for admiration. Embassies and High Commissions hold Open Days and everyone enjoys Canberra's month-long garden party.

A CITY OF GARDENS

The landscaping and planting of Canberra's parks, gardens and thoroughfares has been carefully planned and implemented. The Australian Capital Territory has four distinct seasons: a hot dry summer, crisp clear autumn, cold sometimes icy winter and bright, warm spring. This means that the gardener has plenty of choice of Australian native plants or exotics or both, and the two million people who visit Canberra each year are amazed and delighted by the variety and beauty of garden designs.

The wonderful Australian National Botanic Gardens occupy a 50 ha site on the slopes of Black Mountain. Here, plants from all parts of Australia are displayed in theme areas easily reached by a network of paths and tracks – the Rainforest Walk, Rock Garden and Aboriginal Trail are particularly popular with visitors. There is a fine herbarium and the gardens also serve as a venue for continuing research into plant life.

COLOURS OF CANBERRA

What is the best time to visit Canberra? Many prefer the charms of spring and gardens brocaded with blooms. Others enjoy summer, when cool green foliage provides shade. There are those who love winter's red-berried evergreens and branches silver with frost. But connoisseurs say Canberra's golden autumns, when leaves warm, then glow, then blaze – like the trees on Aspen Island, setting of the Carillon (*inset left*) – are most gorgeous of all.

Autumn gilds trees on the shores of Lake Burley Griffin.

Dawn on Lake Burley Griffin.

A rainforest walk in the Australian National Botanic Gardens.

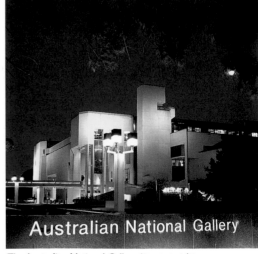

Australian National Gallery

The Australian National Gallery lit up at night.

TIDBINBILLA

The piece of moon-rock shown below can be seen at Tidbinbilla Deep Space Communication Complex, 40 km south-west of Canberra. Operated by Australia for the United States's NASA, Tidbinbilla tracking facility is near Tidbinbilla Nature Reserve, a haven for wildlife.

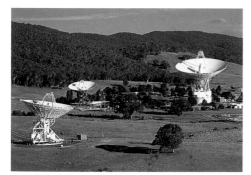

Tidbinbilla Deep Space Communication Complex has displays of spacecraft and space tracking technology.

Colourful figures performing energetic activities ornament the approach to Questacon.

Cockington Green, a miniature world at Gungahlin.

The Times Fountain, in Canberra's city centre, Civic.

SIGHTS TO SEE, PLACES TO GO

There are several places from which Canberra can be viewed in all its logical elegance. The Telstra Tower allows an eagle's eye panorama from one of the observation platforms on the spire that rises 195 m above the 812 m high summit of Black Mountain. Mount Ainslie gives good views of city and lake, while Parliament House and the southern shores of the lake can be seen from Red Hill.

Lake Burley Griffin and the buildings within the Parliamentary Triangle – Parliament House, the Australian National Gallery, High Court of Australia and Australian National Library – are prime objectives in any tour of Canberra. Also by the lake, Questacon (the National Science and Technology Centre) is a must-visit for everyone interested in hands-on interactive displays.

Lake Burley Griffin and its surrounds offer endless opportunities for sailing, cruises, picnicking and cycling. Commonwealth Park allows views of the lake, the Captain Cook Memorial Water Jet and the Carillon on Aspen Island. Black Mountain is the site of the superb National Botanic Gardens, while the Australian Institute of Sport, with its fine training facilities and splendid sculptures (*inset left*) can be toured.

For some, the Australian War Memorial with its memories and displays is the highlight of a Canberra tour. For others, the miniature buildings of Cockington Green, or the realistic reproductions of the National Dinosaur Museum nearby are not to be missed.

Shopping, restaurants, theatre, a casino, and outdoor activities – Canberra can supply all of them and more.

Telstra Tower stands 195 m above Black Mountain.

A display at the National Dinosaur Museum at Gold Creek.

An aerial view of the Australian Institute of Sport.

Inside the impressive Australian War Memorial.

35

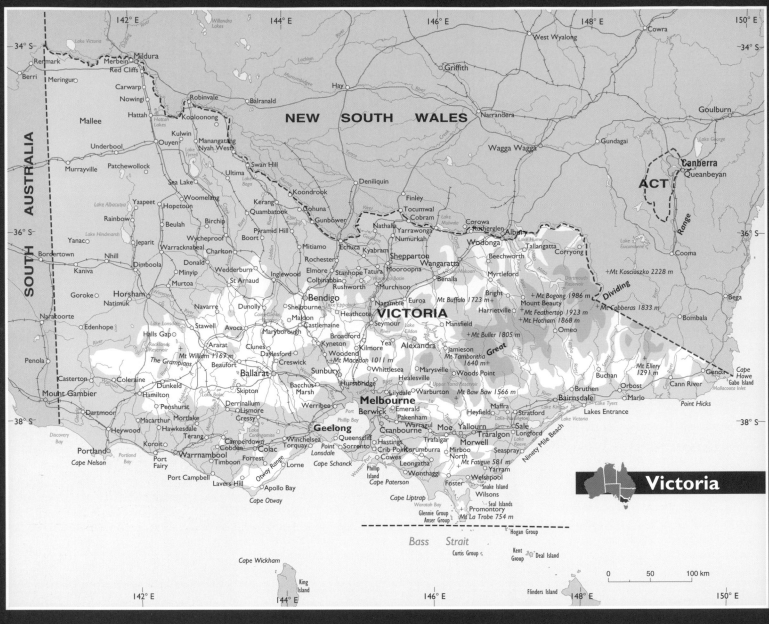

Victoria

The Twelve Apostles, Port Campbell National Park.

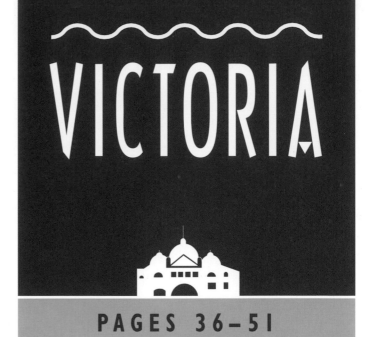

VICTORIA

Victoria occupies less than 3% of the area of Australia, yet it encompasses a wide variety of landscapes and life-styles. Places of quietude and places of excitement, surf skiing and snow skiing, classy hotels and bush cabins, wild country and tamed country – you name it, Victoria has it.

PAGES 36–51

Melbourne, the capital of Victoria, is one of the great cities of the world. It is elegant, it is multicultural, and it offers the latest in entertainment and international trends while retaining its very Australian identity. Within easy reach of Melbourne, the Dandenong Ranges, Phillip Island, and the Mornington and Bellarine Peninsulas reward exploration. Further afield are such adventures as climbing the Grampians (*above*), travelling the Murray on a paddlewheeler, bushwalking and wildlife-watching in national parks, and a feast of other holiday delights.

MELBOURNE & SURROUNDS

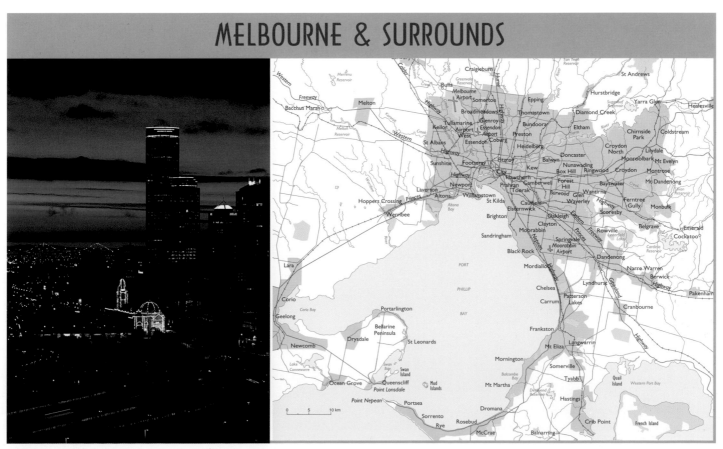

Melbourne at night, with Flinders St Station in the middle distance.

Flinders Street Station, a Melbourne landmark.

Melbourne is built on comparatively level ground, and its suburbs stretch for great distances. The city has a population of nearly three million, yet it is noted for courtesy and friendliness – perhaps the many green spaces offer opportunities to relax from big-city stress. Melbourne is a great place to shop. It is also a culturally aware city, with plenty of theatre groups, a lively music scene, and magnificent artistic venues in the Victorian Arts Centre and the National Gallery of Victoria.

A Venetian-style gondola on the Yarra.

BATMAN'S TOWN

In 1835, the Aboriginal people who had lived along the banks of the Yarra River for many thousands of years allowed John Batman and a group of settlers to found a village there. The following year "Batmania", as Batman's followers called the hamlet, was officially named Melbourne, and in 1850 it became the capital of the new colony of Victoria.

The gold discoveries of the 1850s provided the wealth to construct the gracious buildings typical of Melbourne. Today's glittering city towers have simply added to the elegance of this lovely Victorian city.

CITY ON THE YARRA RIVER

The Yarra River winds serenely to Port Phillip Bay through Melbourne, much of its course bordered by green spaces. In the imposing stretch that sweeps into the city centre between Morell Bridge and Princes Bridge, shown in the picture at right, the Yarra is bordered by parklands and sporting facilities. Tree-lined Alexandra Avenue follows its course on the south bank and Batman Avenue on the north bank. To explore the Yarra, drive one of these avenues, stopping to enjoy the sights.

Bicycles to ride along the many riverside tracks can be hired below Princes Bridge and in South Yarra. Take a river cruise (departing from Princes Walk, below Princes Bridge), or hire a canoe at Riversdale or Fairfield Park boathouse. If none of these suits, just wander along the Yarra's banks, admiring the river and the views of the city skyline.

The Yarra River winds through Melbourne. On its south bank the Royal Botanic Gardens enclose Government House; on the north bank lie a variety of sporting venues.

The Yarra reflects the lights of Melbourne city.

TEMP °C	J	F	M	A	M	J	J	A	S	O	N	D
MAX	26	26	24	20	17	14	13	15	17	20	22	24
MIN	14	14	13	11	8	7	6	7	8	9	11	13

Population: Over 3 million (70% of the population of Victoria).
Rainfall: All months of the year. January & February have fewest rainy days.

WHERE IS IT?

1	St Kilda Brkwater & Pier	10	Lygon & Victoria Sts
2	Albert Park Lake	11	Exhibition Centre
3	Vic Arts Centre	12	Melbourne Central
4	Southgate Complex	13	City Baths
5	St Pauls Cathedral	14	Carlton
6	Carlton Gardens	15	Williamstown
7	Port Phillip Bay	16	Port Melbourne
8	Crown Casino	17	Yarra River
9	State Library	18	Flagstaff Gardens

ON THE YARRA'S SOUTH BANK

On the south bank of the Yarra, between the river and the Victorian Arts Centre and National Gallery, is Southgate complex, a wonderful place to eat, shop, drink coffee or promenade the riverside walks. The choice of cuisine here ranges from the delicacies of the International Food Court to à la carte dining at one of the complex's fine restaurants. A graceful footbridge connects one end of Southgate to Flinders St Station on the north bank, while historic Princes Bridge spans the river at the other end. The Crown Hotel and Casino, downstream of Southgate, attracts many to its facilities and lavish entertainments.

The graceful spire of the Victorian Arts Centre.

The imposing tower of the Crown Hotel and Casino.

MOVING AROUND MELBOURNE

Melbourne's public transport system, The Met, consists of trams, buses and trains, and one ticket allows travel on all three. Melbourne's famous trams (*below*) cover city and suburbs (drivers must give way to trams at all times, and, at signposted intersections in the city, pause on their left before turning right). The City Circle Tram offers a free, 30-minute tour of the central city every 10 minutes between 10 a.m. and 6 p.m. A City Explorer bus leaves Flinders Street Station every hour between 10 a.m. and 4 p.m. From the same station, the hub of the city's rail system, an underground loop serves the centre of the city.

Southgate on the banks of the Yarra. Inset: Sculpture "Ophelia", 1992, Deborah Halpern.

Melbourne Central includes an old shot tower.

Gog and Magog guard Royal Arcade.

LET'S GO SHOPPING!

For the buyer, the browser, the just-looker and the shopaholic, Melbourne is full of irresistible opportunities. Boutiques abound in locations such as stylish Royal Arcade and the charming Block Arcade. A multi-story alternative is the splendour of 234 Collins Street (*right*). Several major department stores open onto Bourke Street Mall, while Swanston Street Walk encourages shoppers to take time out for coffee. Glittering Melbourne Central encloses both an historic shot tower and the treasures of Daimaru department store. However, for a real Melbourne experience, try the Queen Victoria Market and the nearby Arts and Crafts Centre.

Bourke Street Mall.

THE GARDEN CITY

Melbourne has so many notable parks that only a few can be mentioned here. The Royal Botanic Gardens covers 36 hectares with flowerbeds, lawns and shady trees, and features lakes alive with waterfowl. Nearby King's Domain and Queen Victoria Gardens are home to such Melbourne landmarks as the Shrine of Remembrance and the Myer Music Bowl and to a wealth of statues and monuments. Carlton Gardens houses the stately Exhibition Buildings, and Fitzroy Gardens boasts Cook's Cottage and a charming Conservatory full of flowers and statuary (*inset above right*).

Feeding waterfowl at the Royal Botanic Gardens.

EATING OUT IN MELBOURNE

Whatever cuisine the would-be diner craves, it can be found in Melbourne, where food from around the world is an art form. Indeed, there are tours available for keen "foodies". There are plenty of five-star restaurants, and many other places serving marvellous meals at reasonable prices. Inner city dining includes Chinatown, centred on Little Bourke St. The elegant Colonial Tramcar Restaurant tours the city while diners indulge. Inner city suburbs including Carlton, Fitzroy, St Kilda, Richmond and Footscray offer everything from fish and chips to sashimi.

Lygon Street is ready and waiting to serve fine food.

CULTURE IS FOR EVERYONE

From grand opera and classic theatre to jazz in pubs and stand-up comedy, entertainment is easy to find in Melbourne. An entertainment guide published with the *Age* newspaper each Friday lists what is on where. The imposing Victorian Arts Centre, the Princess Theatre, Her Majesty's and the Athenaeum stage a wide range of productions. A very popular International Comedy Festival is held each April. Big, crowd-pulling events may be held at the Concert Hall at the Arts Centre or at the National Tennis Centre, while the Zoo and the Myer Music Bowl host outdoor concerts on warm summer evenings.

Entertainment for all at the Victorian Arts Centre.

MELBOURNE ZOO

Opened in 1862, Melbourne's splendid zoo is home to more than 350 different sorts of animals. Highlights of a zoo visit can include seeing Lowland Gorillas, Sumatran Tigers and Koalas, and a visit to the Butterfly House.

The rare Lowland Gorilla can be seen at Melbourne Zoo.

The National Tennis Centre (foreground) and Melbourne Cricket Ground (centre right).

SPORTS-MAD AND LOVING IT

Melburnians are great sports lovers and flock to events such as November's Melbourne Cup, the Grand Prix motor race, the Australian Open tennis each January and Test and one-day cricket. However, it is Australia's very own football code, "Aussie Rules", which holds the city in thrall over the winter months. Most sports are represented in Melbourne, and the city boasts four of the Top 100 golf courses in the world.

The Victorian Houses of Parliament, begun in 1856.

SMTH

A colonial mansion, Como House dates to 1847.

CONNECTING WITH THE PAST

Buildings such as the Old Customs House, the Houses of Parliament, the Princess Theatre, the Windsor Hotel and St Pauls Cathedral epitomise Melbourne's historic heritage. History enthusiasts should also visit Maritime Park and the barque *Polly Woodside*. The Old Melbourne Gaol, which exhibits Ned Kelly's armour (*right*), and the National Museum of Victoria are wonderful places to spend a day. Tasma Terrace, behind Parliament House, is the headquarters of the National Trust, which is responsible for properties such as Como House, in South Yarra, and Ripponlea, in Elsternwick, both open to the public.

The Princess Theatre was opened in 1886.

BY PORT PHILLIP BAY

Melbourne's bayside suburbs are full of possibilities for fun and entertainment. Williamstown has a maritime tradition and features the enthralling Scienceworks complex (*right*). St Kilda is a traditional resort famed for food, Luna Park and a pier used as a promenade and marina. Bathing boxes add colour to the family beach at Brighton.

Yachts at St Kilda Pier.

Brighton bathing boxes

Coastal vegetation, Phillip Island.

Australian Fur-seal underwater.

PHILLIP ISLAND

San Remo lies 120 km down the Bass Highway to the south-east of Melbourne. A bridge connects the town to Newhaven, on Phillip Island, which lies across the entrance to Westernport Bay. Most popular drawcard on this scenic island are the Little Penguins (*right*) which return from the sea to Summerland Beach each evening. Viewers watch the floodlit "parade" from designated areas. At the south-west tip of Phillip Island, Australian Fur-seals can be viewed from telescopes on The Nobbies, or seen close up from a ferry from Cowes, the island's main town. Koalas are displayed at the Koala Conservation Centre.

Some of Australia's most enjoyable places are within a couple of hours' drive from Melbourne. It may take a comparatively short time travelling along Victoria's excellent roads to reach a destination such as Phillip Island or the Central Highlands, but it is usually worth staying at least overnight. The Yarra Valley, for example, produces fine wines and some of the world's great cheeses, and a food-lovers' tour of the region can extend enjoyably over a considerable time.

Little Penguins nest on Phillip Island.

The final section of the Mornington Peninsula forms a barrier between Port Phillip Bay and the Southern Ocean.

MORNINGTON PENINSULA

The Mornington Peninsula forms the eastern arm of Port Phillip Bay. Along the bay side lie resorts such as Mount Martha, Dromana, Rosebud Rye, Sorrento and Portsea, easily accessed by the Nepean Highway. Take the chairlift to Arthur's Seat, near Dromana, for views of the peninsula. Point Nepean National Park, bordering Bass Strait, offers surf beaches and rugged scenery. The fertile hinterland, which has excellent wineries and plenty of restaurants, art galleries and craft shops, is well worth leisurely exploration.

Cape Schanck, southern tip of the peninsula, from the air.

Cape Woolamai, on Phillip Island's south-eastern tip.

An aerial view of Point Nepean, site of an historic fort.

THE DANDENONGS

Only 50 km from Melbourne, the beautiful Dandenong Ranges are renowned for majestic stands of forest and for glorious gardens, such as the Rhododendron Gardens at Olinda (*below*). Mt Dandenong is 633 m high: an after-dark visit to the summit is rewarded with a stunning view of the sparkling lights of Melbourne. The lush green gullies of Dandenong Ranges National Park, where Mountain Ash trees tower over tree ferns (*below right*), harbours Superb Lyrebirds and a wealth of other wildlife. Puffing Billy, a restored steam train that is possibly the Dandenongs' best-loved feature, chugs and toots between Belgrave and the Emerald Lakeside Park every day of the year except for Christmas and fire-ban days.

HEALESVILLE SANCTUARY

Surrounded by forested ranges and the wine-producing country of the Yarra Valley, Healesville is 65 km along the Maroondah Highway from Melbourne. Healesville Sanctuary, on Badger Creek five minutes from the town, has one of Australia's best displays of native fauna, mostly kept in bushland settings.

Highlights of the sanctuary are the Platypus project (open for a limited time each day), the nocturnal and reptile displays, the colonies of breeding waterbirds, walk-through kangaroo enclosures, the Koala colony and a thrilling exhibition featuring free-flying birds of prey.

A forest stream near Marysville.

THE CENTRAL HIGHLANDS

Some 37 km to the north-east of Healesville is the lovely town of Marysville, a wonderful base from which to explore the Central Highlands, which are the foothills of the Great Dividing Range. Nearby Steavenson Falls, Victoria's highest, are floodlit each night. Cathedral Range State Park is just 10 km north-west of Marysville and Lady Talbot Drive loops past the area's scenic places. In winter, cross-country skiers stay at Marysville to enjoy the slopes at Lake Mountain, 21 km to the east.

This Wedge-tailed Eagle is part of a Healesville display.

A member of Healesville's Koala colony.

The Twelve Apostles, remnants of once-mainland cliffs.

Victoria's untamed south-western coastline was opened up by the 1932 completion of the Great Ocean Road. Until this master-feat of engineering and manual labour came into being, much of the coast could be seen only from the sea, from vessels passing a shoreline with the ominous title, the Shipwreck Coast. In the late 1980s, an added section of the Road opened up the heart of the Otway Ranges. Evidence of the region's role in Australian history, welcoming seaside resorts, great surf beaches, magic rainforests and magnificent coastal scenery make south-western Victoria a premier holiday destination.

GREAT OCEAN ROAD

Take the Great Ocean Road for one of the great experiences of a lifetime, for it is a pathway to some of Australia's most scenic coastline and forests.

A memorial to those who fell in World War I, the road was carved, by returned servicemen, from the limestone cliffs bordering the Southern Ocean. Begun in 1919 it was not completed until 1932. Its best-known section borders Port Campbell National Park, where the coastal rock has been sculptured into caves, arches, islands and stacks by the relentless ocean.

The section of the road between Lorne and Apollo Bay takes the traveller to a series of beautiful beaches and picturesque headlands on one side and the glories of the Otway Ranges, with their rainforested valleys, streams and waterfalls, on the other.

For those unable to see the south-western coast by car, there are regular bus services from Geelong to Warrnambool.

BELLARINE PENINSULA

Geelong is the gateway to the Bellarine Peninsula, which guards the western entrance to Port Phillip Bay. The port of Geelong has long been associated with shipping wool from the Western Districts, and the National Wool Museum (*below right*), sited in a bluestone wool store, offers a fascinating glimpse into Australia's pastoral industry. Queenscliff, 31 km east of Geelong, looks out over the treacherous Rip at the entrance to Port Phillip and was originally a sea pilot's base. At Fort Queenscliff, built in 1882, there are the Black and the White lighthouses and fortifications. A passenger ferry operates across Port Phillip Bay between Queenscliff and Portsea, and a vehicular ferry from Queenscliff to Sorrento. Harold Holt Marine Reserve is popular with scuba divers.

RESORTS AND BEACHES

The Surf Coast Highway connects Geelong to Torquay, bypassing the peninsula. Surfing is big business along this coast and Bells Beach, just south of Torquay, was proclaimed a Surfing Reserve in 1973. The Bells Easter Surfing Competition is the longest-running professional surfing contest in the world.

Visit Anglesea for its beach and a round of golf where the greens are shared with kangaroos. The Great Ocean Road allows good access to the coast from Anglesea onwards. Aireys Inlet and Lorne look inland to Angahook-Lorne State Park, noted for heathland birds and native orchids, waterfalls and cascades.

After Apollo Bay, the Great Ocean Road swings away from the coast and runs through the wonderful Otway National Park at the southern end of the Otway Ranges. Cape Otway marks the western end of Bass Strait. Its lighthouse was completed in 1848.

Great Ocean Road near Lorne.

A top pro surfing event is held at Bells Beach annually.

Aireys Inlet, Split Point and the lighthouse built in 1891.

PORT CAMPBELL NATIONAL PARK

The Twelve Apostles.

The spectacular landforms of the south-western Victorian coastline have been sculptured by waves undercutting the limestone cliffs, forming arches that eventually collapse to leave stacks and islands. Attractions in Port Campbell National Park include London Bridge, whose landward arch collapsed in 1990, the Twelve Apostles, Loch Ard Gorge, Mutton Bird Island and The Arch.

London Bridge today.

Boardwalks and platforms allow viewing of dramatic coastal features in Port Campbell National Park. For the energetic visitor, fishing tracks lead down to secluded beaches where Little Penguins come ashore at sunset.

Many vessels foundered on the reefs and cliffs of the Port Campbell coast, some with great loss of life. The emigrant ship *Cataraqui* sank in 1845 with the loss of 406 lives; the *Admella*, with the loss of 94 lives, in 1859; the *Loch Ard*, with 52 lives lost, in 1878. The Loch Ard Museum, Port Campbell, displays shipwreck mementos.

The indented coast.

CASCADES AND TREE FERNS

Angahook-Lorne State Park follows the Otway Ranges from Aireys Inlet to Kennett River. Walking tracks lead through cool temperate rainforest to waterfalls (cascading Erskine Falls is only five minutes' stroll from a car park) and there are plenty of good bushland picnic places and ocean swimming beaches.

Otway National Park, south and west of Apollo Bay, has few towns. Its forests are dominated by towering Mountain Ash, which may grow up to 100 m in height. Waterfalls, wallabies (*left*), possums and many bird species add to the interest of the forest.

Melba Gully State Park is a 48 ha reserve that was once the site of two sawmills. Today ancient Myrtle Beech, some possibly 2000 years old, stand amid ferns and mosses. At night, visitors may see glow worms, actually luminescent fly larvae.

Flagstaff Hill Maritime Village, Warrnambool.

TWO WESTERN PORTS

The main centre for the Shipwreck Coast is Warrnambool, standing on Lady Bay 263 km south-west of Melbourne. It is an elegant town with beautiful parks and gardens, where Flagstaff Hill Maritime Village is well worth visiting. There is a whale-viewing platform at Logans Beach, east of town, from which Southern Right Whales can be seen passing between May and October.

About 30 km west of Warrnambool, Port Fairy is home to a large fishing fleet. An old-world seaport full of National-Trust-classified buildings, it holds an award-winning Folk Festival each March, and a Spring Music Festival each October.

Erskine Falls are an attraction of the Otway Ranges.

Tree-ferns and Eastern Yellow Robin.

Relics of Australia's past in Swan Hill.

The north-western and central region of Victoria offer highlights such as the scenic Grampians and climber-challenging Mt Arapiles, rising from plains that, in springtime, become wildflower gardens. The Mallee is mecca for birdwatchers and plant enthusiasts: it is bounded to the north by the mighty Murray River, curving lazily in its middle course, bordered by orchards and enjoyed by holiday-makers. In central Victoria, goldrush towns offer historic and other delights.

A reminder of the way things were in the Mallee.

THE GRAMPIANS

Amongst Victoria's most spectacular natural features, the four ranges that make up the Grampians stretch for 90 km north of the town of Dunkeld. After entering through Halls Gap, it is a short distance to the Wonderland Range that has some of the area's best walking trails. It is also worth visiting Brambuk Living Cultural Centre and learning about Aboriginal life in the area. Wallaroo Wildlife Park and Zumstein's Recreation Area are good places to meet native animals, and birdwatchers will find around 200 species to discover. Over 900 species of native plants grow in the Grampians National Park and in spring and summer there are plenty of wildflowers to be seen.

While the Grampians attracts many bushwalkers, Mt Arapiles, 33 km west of Horsham, has more than 2000 different routes up its rock faces (*above left*) and is a target for climbers from all over the world. However, the less energetic visitor can drive to the summit.

Central western Victoria offers many peaceful rural scenes such as this one.

MacKenzie Falls, one of the Grampians' many attractions.

THE MAGIC OF THE MALLEE

The north-western corner of Victoria, the Mallee, was once covered by many-trunked, drought-tolerant eucalypts called mallees. Today much has been cleared for sheep and crops, but there are still extensive reserves, notably Wyperfeld National Park, the Big Desert Wilderness and Murray-Sunset National Park. Ouyen or Mildura can serve as a base to tour the Mallee and to hope for a glimpse of the rare, ground-living Mallee Fowl (*right*), whose eggs are incubated in a mound of sand carefully tended by the male. In spring, the Mallee puts on a marvellous show of wildflowers.

Viewing the Grampians from the Balconies (the Jaws of Death).

Mt Arapiles offers some of Australia's best rock-climbing.

CITIES OF A GOLDEN AGE

In the 1850s, rich deposits of surface gold were discovered near where Ballarat, Bendigo and a number of other towns now stand. Until the 1890s, these gold towns were centres of affluence and culture in Victoria, and the wealth they produced paid for their magnificent civic buildings. Ballarat, 110 km along the Western Freeway from Melbourne, re-creates the days of the goldrushes at Sovereign Hill. Visit this lovely city in March for the Begonia Festival centred on the spacious Botanic Gardens. Bendigo also has many splendid buildings and monuments (*left*). The restored Central Deborah Gold Mine is open daily and the city's strong Chinese associations are celebrated in the Golden Dragon Museum. Stawell, Daylesford and Castlemaine are other gold towns.

Ballarat's Botanic Gardens have a March begonia display.

Red Hill Gully Diggings, at Sovereign Hill, Ballarat.

A Cobb & Co coach waits for passengers in Sovereign Hill, where a goldrush town of the 1850s has been re-created.

THE MURRAY RIVER WEST OF ECHUCA

The Murray's often meandering course (*above*) from Echuca to the South Australian border is full of historic interest. Towns such as Swan Hill and Echuca are living monuments to the great riverboat days. Take a nostalgic cruise on a paddlesteamer (*right*), drive interstate over the bridge at Mildura (*above right*), go fishing, birdwatching or bushwalking, or relax under a river gum tree.

Autumn foliage in the north-east.

Poplars march across a landscape in the foothills of Victoria's Alps.

The Great Dividing Range stretches from the high plains of Victoria's north-east, its peaks snow-capped in winter. Alpine National Park, Victoria's largest reserve, links with New South Wales's Kosciuszko National Park to encompass a large area of Australia's alpine areas. This country starred in the film, *The Man from Snowy River* – its scenery is amongst Australia's most dramatic. Eastwards of the Alps, travellers should try the coastal magic of Croajingolong National Park and the Mallacoota area.

THE MIGHTY MURRAY

The Murray River can be traced back to a source near Mt Kosciuszko. The Murray Valley Highway follows the river from Robinvale in the north-west to Corryong, in the foothills of the Australian Alps.

For much of the 1800s, riverboats on the Murray transported passengers, timber, wool and other goods. Until the 1880s, Echuca was Australia's leading inland port, one of several towns where fleets of paddlesteamers docked at long wharves of locally-cut River Red Gum. Today, Echuca's old port area re-creates the roaring riverboat days.

Paddlesteamers, houseboats, canoes and rafts (*above right*) are all great ways to travel the Murray and to soak up the atmosphere of the river. Canoes can be hired at Echuca or further east at Yarrawonga, on the western edge of Lake Mulwala. When exploring the Murray, keep in mind that the backwaters, wetlands and woodlands along its course offer scenic beauty and abundant wildlife.

TO THE RIVER'S SOURCE

Upstream of Echuca and Lake Mulwala is Victoria's main wine-making area, centred on Rutherglen, on the Murray Valley Highway 9 km from the river. Eastwards again is the major centre of Wodonga, whose twin city, Albury, stands in NSW on the Murray's northern bank. The Murray Valley Highway follows the river past Lake Hume, ideal for all sorts of water sports, to Corryong, in the foothills of the Alps. In this charming town lies the grave of Jack Riley, who is supposed to have inspired the poem "The Man from Snowy River".

An aerial view of the twin cities of Albury and Wodonga.

The Murray River emerges from the foothills of the Victorian Alps near Corryong.

THE COASTAL NORTH-EAST

Croajingolong National Park, in the north-eastern corner of Victoria, has 100 km of unspoiled beaches and surrounds scenic Mallacoota Inlet. The park is a major feature of an area with excellent camp sites. Towns such as Genoa, Buchan and Orbost are pleasant bases from which to explore the inlet, or visit Snowy River National Park or Errinundra National Park, a rich temperate rainforest area.

Camping grounds at Mallacoota.

A catch of Murray crays.

Sunrise on the Victorian Alps.

WINTER SPORTSFIELDS

Victoria's spectacular Alps, part of the Great Dividing Range, are also known as the High Country. While not high by world standards (Mt Bogong at 1986 m is Victoria's highest peak), they offer excellent snow sports in winter and scope for many summertime activities as well. Two national parks, Alpine and Mt Buffalo, protect the fragile alpine environments, and co-exist with high mountain ski resorts and with all-seasons towns situated in the foothills.

Mt Buller is about 220 km from Melbourne via Mansfield and caters for beginners to advanced skiers. Mt Buffalo, about 330 km from the capital via Myrtleford is a family-oriented resort with good cross-country trails. Falls Creek, about 350 km from Melbourne, offers runs for skiers of all standards. Mt Hotham, about 365 km from Melbourne, is for experienced downhill skiers as well as cross-country enthusiasts. All offer ski hire and instruction.

In winter the Victorian Alps rise in stark, snow-clad majesty.

On the slopes in the Victorian Alps.

NORTH-EASTERN ADVENTURES

The skiing season opens on the Queen's Birthday weekend each June and closes in October. Spring and summer adventures in the High Country include trout-fishing, sailing, water-skiing, canoeing, birdwatching, climbing, bushwalking or just marvelling at the spring alpine wildflowers. Horseback riding is popular (*above*) and horses can be hired in many towns or resorts in the area.

Beechworth, once the centre of the Ovens goldmining region, is situated 24 km off the Ovens Highway past Wangaratta. It is beautifully preserved, declared a "notable town" by the National Trust. Bright, another gold town in the Ovens Valley, famed for deciduous trees which, every autumn, make sure the town lives up to its name, is a centre for hang-gliders and alpine visitors.

A Snow Gum in winter.

The colourful foliage of deciduous trees spangles the town of Bright in autumn.

A Snow Gum in summer, Alpine National Park.

Volunteer surf lifesaving team on the Ninety Mile Beach.

Australia's largest system of inland waterways, wonderful beaches, rolling green pastures covered with grazing cattle, the foothills of the High Country, historic townships and the magnificence of Wilsons Promontory – south-eastern Victoria provides endless opportunities for exploration and enjoyment. After a long day spent fishing, sailing, surfing, wandering along the beach or through the forest, the holiday-maker can relax over a meal that includes the delicacies for which the area is famous.

GIPPSLAND

The Latrobe Valley of West Gippsland produces brown coal and Bass Strait oil, but its industrial centres such as Sale, 200 km east of Melbourne, are surrounded by lush green farmlands. The area north of Warragul and Drouin is famous for "gourmet deli" food, including cheeses, venison and berry fruits.

The South Gippsland Highway passes the Strzelecki Ranges and is the quickest way to reach Wilsons Promontory. Most travellers use this route to South Gippsland and the Gippsland Lakes. There are more than 400 sq km of waterways lying behind the sand barrier of Ninety Mile Beach.
This is an area for surfing, swimming, sailing, fishing, birdwatching and family holidays.

Right inset:
Australian
Pelicans at
Lakes Entrance.

An historic cottage at Sale, Gippsland's administrative centre.

The Den of Nargun, in Mitchell River National Park.

TOWNS AND NATIONAL PARKS

Sale, at the junction of the Princes and South Gippsland Highways, and Bairnsdale, where the Princes and Omeo Highways meet, are good bases from which to explore Gippsland. Lakes Entrance, Paynesville, on Lake Victoria about 18 km south of Bairnsdale, and Metung, on Lake King, are centres for fishing, birdwatching and boating (*right*) on the Lakes.

The Gippsland Lakes National Park includes the coastal bushland of Sperm Whale Head peninsula and Rotamah Island. There is a bird observatory on the island, which can only be reached by boat. North-west of Bairnsdale, Mitchell River National Park is known for gorges, rainforests, and, on Woolshed Creek, the Den of Nargun, a cavern said to be the lair of a legendary, half-stone monster.

Ninety Mile Beach, broken at Lakes Entrance, bars the Gippsland Lakes from Bass Strait and the Tasman Sea.

Temperate rainforest in Tarra-Bulga National Park.

THE STRZELECKI RANGES

Strzelecki was a Polish nobleman who was the first European to venture into the highlands of South Gippsland. The remaining old-growth forests between the Latrobe Valley and the coast, preserved in places such as Tarra-Bulga National Park, are worth visiting. They are amongst the few remaining refuges of the endangered Leadbeater's Possum, which was presumed extinct until rediscovered in 1961.

Leadbeater's Possum, endangered by forest felling.

Mountain Ash, Strzelecki Ranges, South Gippsland.

WILSONS PROMONTORY

An operational lighthouse stands on South East Point.

Whisky Bay and Picnic Bay.

Along Lilly Pilly Gully Nature Walk.

The town of Yanakie, about 170 km from Melbourne, is the entrance to Wilsons Promontory, the mainland's most southerly point. "The Prom", a national park since 1905, offers an extraordinary assortment of rugged headlands, sandy beaches, flowering heathlands and sheltered rainforest gullies.

The information centre at Tidal River is 32 km along the Nature Drive from the park entrance. Sparkes Lookout and Mt Oberon offer magnificent views across Bass Strait. Wildlife is abundant, and there are more than 100 km of walking tracks, some short and some quite testing.

Squeaky Beach, whose sands squeal when trodden.

VICTORIA

PACIFIC OCEAN

Tasmania

Apollo Bay
Cape Otway

144°E
145°E
146°E
147°E
148°E

Corner Inlet
Snake Island
Cape Liptrap
Waratah Bay
Wilsons
Seal Islands
+ Mt La Trobe 754 m
Glennie Group
Promontory
Anser Group

Hogan Group

Kent Group
Curtis Group
Deal Island

−39°S

Bass   Strait

Inner Sister Island
Outer Sister Island
Palana
Flinders Island
Furneaux
Emita
−40°S
Prime Seal Island
Whitemark
Lady Barron
Group
Chappell Islands
+ Mt Munro 689 m
Cape Barren Island
Clarke Island
Banks Strait

INDIAN

OCEAN

Albatross Island
Three Hummock Island
Hunter Island
Cape Grim
Walker Island
Robbins Island
North Point
Stanley
Cape
Waterhouse Island
Portland
Ringarooma Bay
West Point
Smithton
Port Latta
Noland Bay
Anderson Bay
Marrawah
Table Cape
George Town
Bridport
Gladstone
Eddystone Point
−41°S
Roger River
Wynyard
Bell Bay
Scottsdale
Herrick
Somerset
Burnie
Beauty Point
Derby
Temma
Penguin
Devonport
Port Sorell
George
Ulverstone
Beaconsfield
St Helens
Latrobe
Railton
Mt Barrow 1414 m
Sandy Cape
Savage River
Waratah
Black Bluff
Sheffield
Launceston
Scamander
1339 m +
Deloraine
Westbury
Legges Tor 1572 m
Pieman Head
Mole Creek
Perth
Evandale
St Marys
Cradle Valley
Longford
Stacks Bluff
1528 m
Cradle Mtn 1545 m +
TASMANIA
Cressy
Rossarden
Fingal
Barn Bluff 1559 m +
Poatina
Rosebery
+ Mt Ossa 1617 m
Lake
Conara
Bicheno
Augusta
Zeehan
Campbell Town
Maclean Bay
Eldon Peak 1439 m +
Great Lake
Miena
−42°S
Queenstown
Gormanston
Ross
Tunbridge
Swansea
Coles Bay
Strahan
Derwent Bridge
Bronte
Waddamana
Cape Forestier
Cape Sorell
Park
Freycinet Peninsula
Frenchmans Cap+
Schouten Island
1445 m
Oatlands
Great Oyster Bay
Bothwell
Wayatinah
Ouse
Melton Mowbray
Triabunna
Point Hibbs
Hamilton
+ Quoin Mtn 900 m
Orford
Mt Field West
1439 m +
Maria Island
Boyer
Bridgewater
Richmond
High Rocky Point
Strathgordon
Maydena
Sorell
New Norfolk
Cambridge
Mt Wellington 1271 m+
Marion Bay
Hobart
Forestier Peninsula
Low Rocky Point
Kingston
Huonville
Eaglehawk Neck
−43°S
Snug
Nubeena
Port Arthur
Mt Picton 1327 m +
Franklin
Cygnet
Tasman Peninsula
Geeveston
Storm
Cape Pillar
Dover
Bay
North Bruny
Island
Alonnah
Southport
South Bruny
Island

King Island
Cape Wickham
Currie
Naracoopa
−40°S
Grassy

0   25   50   75   100 km

West Point
Marrawah

Low Rocky Point

Port Davey
Bathurst Harbour
Cox Bight
South West Cape
Maatsuyker Island
South East Cape
D'Entrecasteaux

Tasman

Sea

144°E
145°E
146°E
147°E
148°E

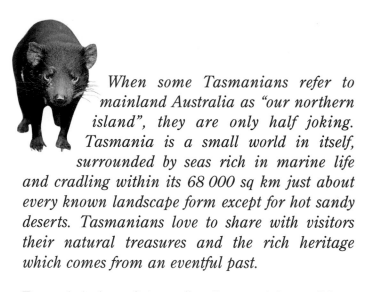

When some Tasmanians refer to mainland Australia as "our northern island", they are only half joking. Tasmania is a small world in itself, surrounded by seas rich in marine life and cradling within its 68 000 sq km just about every known landscape form except for hot sandy deserts. Tasmanians love to share with visitors their natural treasures and the rich heritage which comes from an eventful past.

Tasmania is Australia's smallest State, so it is possible to plan a holiday that takes in many sights in a short time. However, it is best to take time to explore and appreciate, wander from the beaten track and discover little-known treasures side by side with more famous features.

When you are visiting Tasmania, look for wilderness where every step brings discovery, historic ruins where the past comes vividly to life, delightful towns full of charming gardens, and a sea coast unequalled for scenery. The gourmet has a special treat in store, for the island is noted for fresh seafood, splendid farm produce, fine wines and warm hospitality.

Hobart, Tasmania's capital and the second oldest city in Australia, is a beautiful, prosperous city with a superb harbour at the mouth of the Derwent River.

HOBART & SURROUNDS

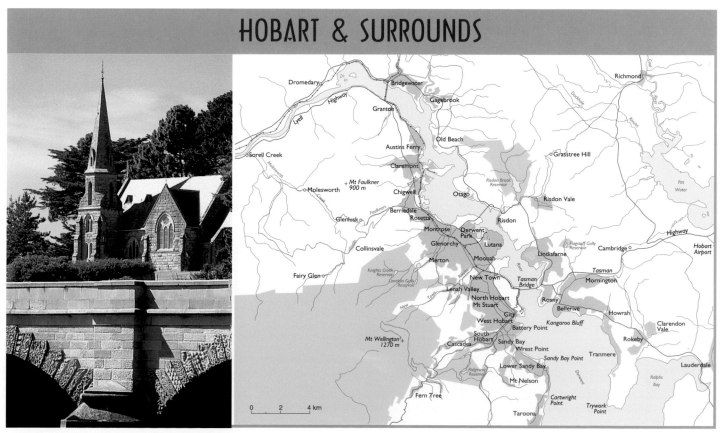

Convicts built the Ross Bridge, which is decorated with Celtic motifs, in 1836.

Hobart's waterfront has great charm.

An aerial view of Hobart and the Derwent River.

Standing on the shores of the Derwent River estuary, beside majestic Mt Wellington, Hobart is a beautiful city in a splendid location. In winter, snow lies on Mt Wellington and Hobart's weather can be bracing, but for most of the year the climate is delightful and walking around the city is a pleasure. There is plenty to see, from the waterfront with its marinas, markets, galleries and restaurants, to historic buildings, monuments and other relics of the city's colourful convict and colonial days.

A CONVICT COLONY

Tasmania was named Van Diemen's Land in 1642 by the Dutch navigator Abel Tasman. In 1803, to protect British sealing and whaling interests, the government in Sydney sent soldiers and convicts to settle on the Derwent River. By 1806, a second settlement had been established at Launceston, in northern Tasmania. The island became self-governing in 1825, but transportation of convicts, especially of those seen as intractable, did not cease until 1853.

Right inset: The Tasman Bridge spans the Derwent River.

CITY ON THE BLUE DERWENT

For many years Hobart Town was a roaring seaport for whalers and sealers. Today the city's waterfront, which centres on Franklin Wharf, is still a focus of activity. Around New Year, Constitution Dock is the place to celebrate the finish of the Sydney to Hobart yacht race. In February all of Sullivans Cove is alive with the Royal Hobart Regatta. On the waterfront, a number of floating food stalls and several excellent restaurants serve some of the best seafood available anywhere.

Battery Point was once a maritime village and today offers endless rewards to a walker: of special interest are the Maritime Museum in Secheron House and the Van Diemen's Land Folk Museum in Hampden Rd. Nearby Salamanca Place dates to the whaling days. Its magnificent restored sandstone warehouses are home to galleries, shops and restaurants. Sandy Bay, site of Hobart's yacht clubs, stretches from Battery Point past the dominating tower of Wrest Point Hotel Casino.

The Tasmanian Museum and Art Gallery behind Constitution Dock.

TEMP °C	J	F	M	A	M	J	J	A	S	O	N	D
MAX	22	22	21	18	15	13	12	13	15	17	19	20
MIN	12	12	11	9	6	5	4	5	6	7	9	11

Population: Approximately 195 000 (41% of the population of Tasmania).
Rainfall: All months of the year. January–February have fewest rainy days.

WHERE IS IT?

1 Princes Park
2 Battery Point
3 Salamanca Place
4 Princes Wharf
5 St Davids Park
6 Parliament Square
7 Murray St Pier
8 Brooke St Pier
9 Sullivans Cove
10 Franklin Square
11 Elizabeth St Pier
12 Tasmanian Museum
13 Constitution Dock
14 Franklin Wharf
15 Victoria Dock

EXPLORING HOBART

It is possible to walk from the centre of Hobart to the summit of Mt Wellington (1270 m) and back on one day, but most people prefer to drive up, then enjoy the views, which are most spectacular at dawn and sunset. The Old Signal Station on Mt Nelson is another good vantage point.

No stay in Hobart would be complete without a Saturday visit to the Salamanca Markets. The National Trust's Saturday morning walking tour explores nearby Battery Point, whose Anglesea Barracks dates to 1811. The Hobart Ghost Tour (summer only) and the Sullivans Cove Tour bring history and geography vividly to life.

Derwent cruises operate from Brooke St Pier at Franklin Wharf and include a very popular expedition to Cadbury's chocolate factory. Some people prefer to make their own tour of Cascade Brewery. Those with a taste for elegance will enjoy Runnymede, a mansion dating to the 1830s, and the Theatre Royal, built in 1837 and Australia's oldest theatre. At St Davids Park, near the city centre, gravestones dating to the colony's earliest days can be viewed.

To the north of the city centre, the Queens Domain harbours both sports fields and the extensive and magnificently planted Royal Tasmanian Botanical Gardens.

Salamanca Place has cafés, markets and an arts centre.

Constitution Dock (left) and Victoria Dock (right).

Winter sunrise on Mt Wellington and the Derwent River.

The suburb of Sandy Bay lies along the Derwent from Wrest Point (casino at bottom right) to Battery Point (top right).

Tasmania is a bushwalker's paradise.

'WARE WILDLIFE!

Around 12 000 years ago, rising sea levels gradually filled Bass Strait, cutting Tasmania off from mainland Australia. The Dingo never reached Tasmania, and the Thylacine and Tasmanian Devil, which disappeared from the mainland after the wild dog's arrival, survived in Tasmania. After Europeans settled on the island, farmers and bounty-hunters exterminated the Thylacine, but the Tasmanian Devil is still quite common there. Other Tasmanian mammals include the Sugar Glider (*above*) the Common Wombat, the Platypus, the Short-beaked Echidna, Bennett's Wallaby, possums and the rare Eastern Barred Bandicoot. Some of these may roam the roads, especially at night, and a little care when driving may save a furry animal from death by car.

The southern half of Tasmania is full of delights for the traveller, some of them immediately available and others only attained after considerable effort. While the forests and falls of Mt Field National Park are within easy reach of Hobart, the mountains and lakes of the south-west are more difficult to reach, but well worth the energy expended to get there. This is World Heritage listed wilderness, remote and magnificent. The south-east corner of the island is notable both for its beauty and for grim relics of the harsh convict system.

Richmond, 26 km from Hobart, has many historic buildings.

Richmond Bridge was built by convicts between 1823 and 1825, and is said to be haunted by the ghost of a murdered overseer.

TOWNS THAT BREATHE HISTORY

Visit towns such as New Norfolk, Bridgewater, Pontville, Brighton and Richmond for fascinating reminders of the convict and colonial days. Richmond, 26 km from Hobart, boasts Australia's oldest bridge and its oldest active Catholic church, St John's, built in 1837.

BEAUTIFUL MT FIELD

A day spent at Mt Field National Park, less than 80 km from Hobart, gives a taste of Tasmania's marvellous scenic delights. The park offers rainforest, alpine moorlands, lakes, abundant wildlife and beautiful waterfalls including easily-accessible Russell Falls and Lady Barron Falls.

The hardy Pandani, a giant heath, can be seen on Mt Field.

Forty m high Russell Falls, in Mt Field National Park.

SOUTH-WESTERN WILDERNESS

Arthur Range, South West National Park.

Franklin-Gordon Wild Rivers National Park.

South West National Park.

The ice-carved, windswept ranges, placid lakes and wild rivers of Tasmania's south-west have been the subject of battles between governments and environmentalists. Today, much of this south-western and western territory is listed as World Heritage Wilderness, and hopefully it will remain so in perpetuity. The Franklin-Gordon Wild Rivers and South West National Parks bring wilderness-lovers and adventurers from all over the world to enjoy nature at its most magnificent. Bushwalking (*left*), angling, rock-climbing, birdwatching, canoeing and just standing awestruck are popular occupations.

Port Davey, South West National Park.

SOUTH-EASTERN SPLENDOUR

The Huon Valley south of Hobart was once known for its massive Huon Pines, then for apple orchards. Today the pines are rare, and wine and Atlantic salmon have been added to apples as products.

A ferry from Kettering travels several times each day to Bruny Island, which guards the entrance to the Huon River. The island has excellent fishing, great beaches and plenty of wildlife, including penguins and the endangered Forty-spotted Pardalote.

Hartz Mts National Park, about 80 km south of Hobart, has been World Heritage Wilderness since 1989. Hartz Peak (1255 m) offers panoramic views, but only the fit should attempt the trek. (Waterproofs and warm clothing are essential for walkers in Tasmania's wild places, where weather conditions may change suddenly. Even in summer, heavy rain is always a possibility.)

THE TASMAN PENINSULA

Port Arthur, which was once a prison, is 100 km from Hobart. Its ruins (the chapel is shown below left) stand on the Tasman Peninsula, which is joined to the Forestier Peninsula (which juts out from Tasmania itself) at narrow Eaglehawk Neck. Fierce dogs were once chained in a line across this 100 m wide isthmus to apprehend would-be escapees. Scenery to be enjoyed nearby includes Pirates Bay, the Devils Kitchen, the Tessellated Pavement and The Blowhole. Between 1830 and 1877, Port Arthur was a dreaded place of punishment. Today it stands as a grim reminder of the many convicts who suffered and sometimes died there. Night-time ghost tours and visits to the Isle of the Dead are very popular with some visitors. Others may prefer finding out if they had convict ancestors from the data base on the Port Arthur museum computer.

The Tessellated Pavement on Pirates Bay.

The Bass Strait ferry at Devonport Dock.

Northern Tasmania has its share of superb wilderness areas, but is also full of rural landscapes remarkable for their calm beauty. It offers some of the best gardens, art and craft galleries and antique shops in Australia. Good food and great restaurants abound, and King Island, off the north-west coast, has become internationally known for its dairy-food delights. While mainland Australia is gripped by summer, cool, green Tasmania is a particularly delightful place to visit.

The suspension bridge at Cataract Gorge, near Launceston.

TRAVELLING TO TASSIE

Many holiday-makers put their vehicles in the hold of a ferry which leaves the TT Lines terminal, Port Melbourne, and makes the voyage to Tasmania overnight. They may travel on the same ferry, or cross Bass Strait by air and meet their vehicle or hire one. Cars, campervans and bus tours are all good ways to see the island, and the athletic may even tour by bicycle. Bed and breakfast accommodation is readily available and of high standard in most towns, and there are plenty of places to dine or snack.

Ferry berths (600 vehicles, 1300 passengers per trip), hire cars and campervans should be booked well in advance, especially in summer.

Rolling green farmland, a crop of oats in the foreground, typical of the country around Devonport, home of the ferry terminus.

LAUNCESTON TO DEVONPORT

Launceston, Tasmania's "northern capital", lies about 60 km up the Tamar River. It is a lovely city, whose nearby attractions include Cataract Gorge and Penny Royal World. It is also the main city on the Tasmania Wine Route.

Take Highway 1 to Devonport, where the ferry from Melbourne docks, investigating such delightful towns as historic Deloraine. In Devonport, don't miss the Maritime Museum and the fine Tiagarra Aboriginal Cultural Centre.

Penny Royal Gunpowder Mill, a Launceston landmark.

Bowerbank Mill Gallery, near Deloraine, was built in 1853.

A mountain hut nestles in the lee of Legges Tor, in Ben Lomond National Park.

Centre below: Crescent Honeyeater on Tasmanian Blue Gum.

The Hazards, a notable feature of Freycinet National Park.

Nineteenth-century Gaol House and Stables in Bicheno.

TOWARDS THE SUNCOAST

Only 50 km south-east of Launceston, beautiful Ben Lomond National Park is a mecca for bushwalkers and rock-climbers in summer and attracts crowds of downhill and cross-country skiers in winter.

Freycinet National Park, situated on a peninsula halfway down the Tasmanian east coast, has plenty of walking tracks. It offers rugged granite headlands and splendid beaches, including the silver sand and azure sea of Wineglass Bay.

The east coast is Tasmania's Suncoast, offering unspoiled beaches, hospitable small resort towns and plenty of excellent, ultra-fresh seafood. St Helens is a particularly good base for scenic cruises, surfing, gamefishing and indulging in fresh-caught seafood. One of the most fascinating towns is the historic port of Bicheno, where scuba divers have taken over from sealers and whalers.

CRADLE MOUNTAIN-LAKE ST CLAIR NATIONAL PARK

Cradle Mountain–Lake St Clair and the Walls of Jerusalem National Parks lie in Tasmania's north-west, and in them are jagged peaks and cliffs gouged by glaciers in a past ice age. Cradle Mountain (seen behind Lake Dove, *left*), rises to 1545 m, and the Overland Track that snakes past it presents 85 km of challenges to walkers. The park also features the marvellous Ballrooms Forest (*above*).

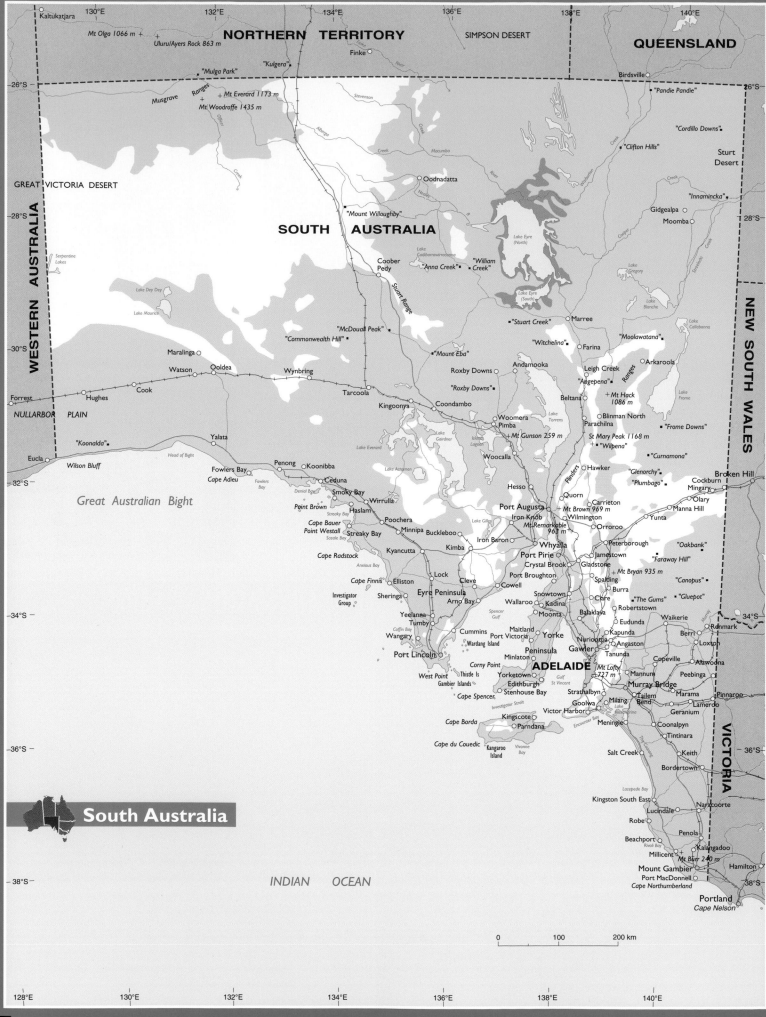

South Australia

South Australia is sometimes called "the Festival State", and South Australians love to share the good things of life with each other and with those fortunate enough to visit them. In the driest State in the driest continent, those who love the desert are well served with spectacular country. In contrast, the south-east corner enjoys the kindness of a Mediterranean climate.

SOUTH AUSTRALIA

PAGES 60–71

South Australia's capital, Adelaide, has long been a centre of cultural life. It is also one of the world's best-laid-out cities, surrounded by parklands, many elegant buildings and the winding charms of the River Torrens. North of Adelaide are the scenic splendours of the Flinders Ranges; to the east the Murray River flows to the bird-haunted wilderness of the Coorong; to the south is Kangaroo Island; and to the west is a sea coast whose unspoiled beauty is equalled by its rich marine life.

Much of the State is arid country, but the fertile lands of the south-east produce wines to vie with the world's best and a wealth of other good things to drink and eat.

South Australia also yields mineral wealth and fine opals. From the depths of the Blue Lake to the salt pans of Lake Eyre, South Australia is a State of exciting contrasts.

ADELAIDE & SURROUNDS

An evening view of Adelaide, capital of South Australia, across Torrens Lake.

Adelaide stands on Gulf St Vincent and is sheltered to the east by the Mt Lofty Ranges. Surveyor-General Light's plan imposed a grid of streets around five squares, surrounded by extensive parklands. This, plus the glorious Mediterranean climate, makes Adelaide a tourist's dream in which landmarks are easy to find and there are plenty of green spaces for relaxation. An early influx of European settlers and continuing migration has fostered Adelaide's multiculturalism. The city hosts an internationally famous Festival of Arts, the largest of its kind in the southern hemisphere, in March of each even-numbered year.

Left: East End Markets.   *Above:* Glenelg Town Hall.

A FREE COLONY

In 1802, Captain Matthew Flinders RN, in *HMS Investigator*, sighted Mt Lofty, then explored Gulf St Vincent. In 1833, the South Australian Association was formed to sell land in South Australia at a price sufficient to finance workers from Britain to migrate there. Thus the colony would be kept free of convict labour. Colonel William Light was to be Surveyor-General and Captain Hindmarsh was to be Governor. *HMS Buffalo* landed settlers at Holdfast Bay in December 1836. Light designed Adelaide as a city of green spaces and ordered streets.

The replica of *HMS Buffalo* shown here is moored in Patawalonga Boat Haven at Glenelg, and contains a seafood restaurant and a museum. A short distance away is the Old Gum Tree, where the colony was proclaimed.

A view across Adelaide Oval, River Torrens, Festival Centre and city centre shows how parklands embrace Adelaide.

GREEN SPACES AND RIVER

Torrens Lake winds between Adelaide and North Adelaide, and a cruise boat or a pedal boat hired near the Festival Centre can be enjoyable ways to explore the waterway. Parklands and sports fields ring the city. A good view of the city can be seen from Montefiore Hill, where stands Light's statue (*inset opposite*).

Adelaide Oval is on the north bank of the river, while Elder Park, with its charming band rotunda, lies between river and Festival Centre. The Adelaide Botanic Gardens, with their nineteenth-century Palm House and huge Bicentennial Conservatory, are north-east of the city centre and are well worth a lengthy visit.

TEMP °C	J	F	M	A	M	J	J	A	S	O	N	D
MAX	29	29	26	22	19	16	15	16	18	21	24	27
MIN	17	17	15	13	10	9	8	8	9	11	13	15

Population: Approximately 1 million (73% of the population of SA).
Rainfall: All months of the year, but most falls from May to October.

Motor vessel cruises tour the Torrens.

The Victoria Square fountain symbolises three rivers.

BROWSING AND GRAZING

Rundle Mall, in the heart of Adelaide city, is a great place to browse and buy, dine or drink coffee. Hindley St is the place for restaurants, pubs and nightclubs; Gouger St for top-of-the-line seafood. Rundle St, at the eastern end of the city, offers boutiques, cafés, restaurants and craft shops, while the East End Markets can be visited from Friday to Sunday. Near Victoria Square are Chinatown, with its many places to eat well, and the busy Central Market. North Adelaide is the place for boutiques and antiques.

ART AND OTHER CULTURE

In a happy circumstance that saves parking traumas and eases tired feet, the popular centres of art and the intellect in Adelaide are close together. The South Australian Museum, Art Gallery and State Library, as well as the stunning Festival Centre, are all on or near North Terrace. This "boulevard of learning" offers other interesting landmarks and places to visit, including a wealth of monuments, Parliament House, Government House, the Adelaide Railway Station and Casino.

Hajek's sculptures decorate the Festival Centre plaza.

Adelaide Railway Station and Casino at night.

The Lavington Bonython Fountain and the Art Gallery.

Rundle Mall, a popular shopping venue.

WHERE IS IT?

1 Elder Park	10 Parliament House
2 University of Adelaide	11 Adelaide Casino, Railway Stn
3 Parklands	12 Convention Centre
4 Art Gallery, Museum	13 Exhibition Centre
5 Government House	14 Adelaide Hills
6 Festival Centre	15 Victoria Square
7 Torrens Lake	16 Montefiore Rd
8 Victoria Pk Racecourse	17 Railway Yards
9 King Wm St, Nth Tce Intersection	

Adelaide is at the hub of a logical and well-kept road system, making it easy to enter and exit the city, and is situated within easy reach of some fascinating and scenic rural attractions. Easy access to the beautiful country of the wine districts would be enough for many people, but to the east Adelaide has the beautiful Mt Lofty Ranges, where festivals of all kinds, always featuring marvellous food, are a way of life. To the west is Gulf St Vincent, with its beaches, water sports and fishing, and south is the Fleurieu Peninsula, and the natural beauty of Kangaroo Island.

Glenelg Jetty at sunset.

GLENELG

For some years after the first British settlers landed on the beach at Glenelg in 1836, immigrants to South Australia had to wade or be carried through the surf to shore. Eventually a jetty 215 m long was built: today it remains a Glenelg landmark.

The 1929 trams (*above*) leave Victoria Square in Adelaide's heart every 15 minutes and deposit passengers in Glenelg around 25 minutes later.

An enjoyable day can be spent swimming, fishing, visiting the Magic Mountain amusement parlour or the *HMS Buffalo* museum, or sampling the dishes of various nations at a wide variety of eating places. During summer, music and other entertainments take place on the lawns and beach where the jetty reaches the shore.

Glenelg Jetty reaches the shore near Glenelg Town Hall and the monument celebrating the arrival of the first British settlers.

THE COAST OF GULF ST VINCENT

A line of beaches stretches south and north of Adelaide. The beaches on the gulf are popular with families because the waters are usually calm and relatively shallow inshore. For big swells, surfers travel south to less protected waters. Only 50 km south of the city centre is Maslins Beach, the first in Australia to sanction nude bathing. Swimmers, divers, windsurfers (*right*), anglers and beach-walkers will all find a beach perfect for their needs.

PORT ADELAIDE

Transport history enthusiasts will revel in Port Adelaide's Maritime Museum, Port Dock Station Railway Museum and the Historical Aviation Museum. In Port Adelaide, just to the north of the city centre, many historic buildings have been restored, and it is the place to embark on pleasure cruises and fishing trips in Gulf St Vincent.

Major Mitchell's Cockatoo and many other parrots can be seen at Adelaide Zoo.

ZOOS

Adelaide Zoo, on Frome Rd, is open every day of the year, breeds rare animals and is internationally renowned for its display of Australian native birds. At Cleland Conservation Park, only 7.5 km south-east of the city, visitors can stroll amongst animals kept in their natural habitats and can meet Koalas face to face.

Historic lighthouse and dockside buildings at Port Adelaide.

IN THE ADELAIDE HILLS

The Adelaide Hills is the name given to the southern Mt Lofty Ranges, from Strathalbyn north to Mt Pleasant. The Mt Lofty Lookout gives an excellent view of Adelaide and the coastal plain, and Mt Lofty Botanic Gardens is only 1.5 km to the south. The Hills are at their best in springtime and when coloured with autumn hues (the town of Aldgate has an Autumn Leaves Festival).

Many of the early settlers in the Mt Lofty Ranges were Germans and their influence is still strong today in towns such as Hahndorf and Lobethal. Hahndorf was named after the captain of the immigrant ship *Zebra*, who in 1839 helped Lutheran families to obtain land. This delightful town full of historic buildings holds several German-style festivals, including Founders Day in January. A trip through the hills towns is rewarding, for each has its own charm and attractions set in countryside of bush, farms and orchards. Birds and native mammals can be seen at Warrawong Sanctuary, near Mylor. Antique enthusiasts and admirers of elegant old buildings should target Strathalbyn. This classified heritage town is situated between two wine districts: the Southern Vales to the west and Langhorne Creek to the east.

A rural scene in the North Mt Lofty Ranges.

Emus feeding in the Adelaide Hills.

Visiting Hahndorf can be like stepping back in history.

THE BAROSSA VALLEY

Tanunda, the gateway to the Barossa.

The Barossa Valley was named by Surveyor-General Light after a battlefield in Spain. Situated about 70 km from Adelaide, it was settled by German families in 1838. Johann Gramp planted the first vines at Jacobs Creek in 1847, and today Barossa vineyards produce world-class vintages. Some of the 50-plus wineries are small and family-owned, others are large and owned by public companies, and nearly all are open to visitors. The Barossa is the scene of some of Australia's most attractive festivals, including the Vintage Festival that begins on Easter Monday each odd-numbered year, the Classic Gourmet Weekend in August or September, and an International Music Festival in September-October. All are worth attending and the valley also offers many art and craft galleries (*right*).

A Barossa Valley landscape.

A bluestone cottage in a vineyard.

In Victor Harbor, a late 19th century bank building.

The Fleurieu Peninsula stretches south of the Southern Vales district. Its other boundaries are Gulf St Vincent, the Backstairs Passage, Encounter Bay and Lake Alexandrina. The peninsula beaches that stretch along the gulf are enjoyed by sailors, swimmers, windsurfers and divers. The ocean beaches are great for surfing and fishing. Inland are historic townships, orchards and vineyards notable for the quality of their wines.

NAMED BY THE FRENCH

In 1802, French captain Nicholas Baudin explored the coastline of South Australia and named the Fleurieu Peninsula in honour of Napoleon's Minister for the Navy. Encounter Bay, on the south-west of the Peninsula, was named after Baudin met Matthew Flinders in the Investigator there. In 1837, whalers set up stations at Encounter Bay, and soon a track to Adelaide was opened up. From the 1850s until the 1880s, Victor Harbor and Goolwa, at the Murray mouth, were major ports.

GRAPEVINES AND ALMOND TREES

McLaren Vale, in the Southern Vales wine and orchard growing area, is less than 40 km from Adelaide. In October, local wineries welcome visitors to the Wine Bushing Festival. In May, seafood and wine are celebrated in From the Sea and the Vines. The first weekend in October sees the Continuous Picnic spread goodwill. Willunga, next district south of McLaren Vale, is noted for its almond orchards: every July, gloriously submerged in flowers, it holds the Almond Blossom Festival. Other peninsula towns worth visiting are Yankalilla, where walkers can enter the Heysen Trail (which ends in the Flinders Ranges) and Cape Jervis, where the trail begins and the Kangaroo Island ferry docks. Port Elliot, on the southern coast of the peninsula, attracts surfers, especially during autumn, and is also the place to try beach-surfing (*left*).

A horse-drawn tram travels the causeway to Granite Island.

VICTOR HARBOR AND GOOLWA

Nature lovers should enjoy Victor Harbor, on Encounter Bay only 84 km from Adelaide. Once a whaling station, it today boasts the SA Whale Centre, which operates a whale information network and tells visitors where whales can be seen along the coast between June and October. Granite Island, which lies between Victor Harbor and the ocean, can be reached on a horse-drawn tram. It is home to a colony of Little Penguins, which can be seen at dusk.

Goolwa, on Lake Alexandrina, once was the port where Murray River cargo was transferred by rail to the docks at Port Elliot. It was bypassed in the 1880s by a railway linking Adelaide direct to Melbourne. Today Goolwa offers cruises of the Murray mouth, Lake Alexandrina and the Coorong, and is a great place for water sports.

McLaren Vale is noted for excellent wines.

Fishing is peaceful and productive on peninsular beaches.

KANGAROO ISLAND

The third-largest island off Australia's shores, Kangaroo Island is 120 km south of Adelaide and easily reached by air from that city. A ferry carries passengers from Glenelg to Kingscote, and vehicular and passenger ferries travel from Cape Jervis to Penneshaw. In the early 1800s, the island was a base for sealers, whalers and escaped convicts. Places to see include the site of first settlement at Kingscote, and Cape Willoughby Lighthouse, 28 km from Penneshaw. The South Coast Road leads to Seal Bay, Cape Gantheaume, and Kelly Hill Caves Conservation Parks, and in to Flinders Chase National Park. Flinders Chase is notable for wildlife, for Cape de Couedic with its Admirals Arch, and for Remarkable Rocks.

Remarkable Rocks at Kirkpatrick Point near Cape de Couedic.

Kelly Hill Caves.

Admirals Arch.

Coastal scenery, Kangaroo Island.

Female Australian Sea-lion and pup.

The Dingo, the fox and the rabbit have never reached Kangaroo Island, so Australian native animals such as kangaroos, bandicoots and possums are plentiful. The Koala and the Platypus have been introduced to the island. The best place to see kangaroos and Koalas is at Rocky River, in Flinders Chase National Park. There are numerous Little Penguin rookeries on the island, including one at Penneshaw, and there is a Discovering Penguins Walk at Kingscote. At American River and Kingscote, pelican feeding takes place each afternoon. Colonies of fur seals and Australian Sea-lions live on the island's southern coast. Ranger-guided tours of Seal Bay introduce visitors to the Australian Sea-lions that use this beach. Birdwatchers will enjoy Murray Lagoon in Cape Gantheaume Conservation Park.

The Murray River flows west from the Victoria–South Australia border to Morgan, then south to enter the Southern Ocean. Regulation of the flow for irrigation and introduced fish species have affected the river and its denizens, but it is a great place to spend a houseboat holiday, fish or wander the towns along the banks. The Riverland, between Blanchetown and Renmark, is an area of orchards and vineyards, bordered to the east by the wheat-growing Murray Mallee. Finally the great river reaches Lake Alexandrina, and the fascinating Coorong.

The Murray River at sunrise.

WATCHING WATERBIRDS

The Murray wanders through its lower course, forming giant C-shapes across the plains. When river flow increases, the rush of water may cut off a half-moon of water called a billabong. The Murray has created many billabongs over the years, and they are wonderful places to watch wildlife, especially waterbirds. The experience will be made even more enjoyable by the use of insect repellent to combat mosquitoes, and by carrying a good pair of binoculars.

Long-legged, long-necked waterbirds to be seen on or near the Murray include ibis, herons and egrets. The Little Black Cormorant (right) and its larger relative the Australian Darter may be spotted perched on dead branches, while ducks are more often seen on the water. The majestic Australian Pelican has become a symbol of the wilderness and beaches of the Coorong.

For much of its South Australian journey, the Murray flows between cliffs and carries many holiday-makers in houseboats.

ALONG THE MURRAY

Many Aborigines lived off the rich bounty of the Riverland. Today, the Murray River provides more than half the water of South Australia's needs. Travellers can explore towns rich in history, relax on a paddlesteamer or houseboat, walk riverside heritage trails and observe wildlife and bushland in national parks and reserves. The Riverland irrigation areas are noted for the produce of market gardens, orchards (particularly citrus and stonefruit) and table and wine grapes.

Waikerie, on the Murray, is well-known to gliding enthusiasts.

A WATER WONDERLAND

The name Coorong comes from an Aboriginal word meaning "narrow neck". It is an inland sea of shallow lagoons extending about 145 km from the Murray mouth to Kingston SE, barred from the sea by the Younghusband Peninsula. With the Lower Murray Lakes, the Coorong has been declared a wetlands of international importance. The largest known breeding colony of Australian Pelicans is found here, and the area has a rich Aboriginal history. Members of the Ngarrindjeri group are willing to show visitors their traditional land and explain their culture.

Australian Pelicans, guardian spirits of the Coorong.

Blue Lake at Mt Gambier averages 77 m in depth. It is bluest from November to March.

THE SOUTH-EAST

Some of South Australia's richest pastoral land lies in the State's south-east, between Bordertown, 274 km south-east of Adelaide on the Dukes Highway, and Mt Gambier, in the south-east corner 440 km from the capital. Meat, wool, cereals and the legendary products of vineyards such as Coonawarra and Padthaway are produced here. South of Bordertown is Naracoorte, where World Heritage listed caves famous for fossilised animals can be explored. Penola, further south, is a pilgrimage site associated with Mother Mary McKillop. Blue Lake at Mt Gambier lies in the crater of an extinct volcano, one of many that once erupted across the region. The Blue Lake Festival takes place each November.

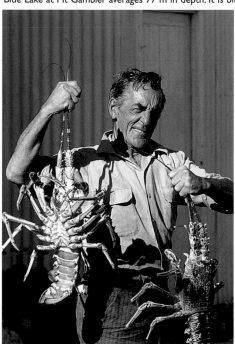

Rock lobsters caught near Kingston.

Cape Northumberland, at Port MacDonnell, with Cape Northumberland Lighthouse at far left.

Hauling in a catch of shrimps in Lake Alexandrina.

THE CRUSTACEAN COAST

From the tasty shrimps of Lake Alexandrina to the large and luscious rock lobsters (crays) of the ocean reefs, gourmet seafood is a hallmark of "the Crustacean Coast". Kingston SE, at the southern end of the Coorong, is noted for its lobster-fishing and for the exuberant Lobster-fest held each January. Further south, Robe is a fishing town with a past as a wool-exporting port (Narraburra Woolshed, near Robe, has demonstrations of working sheep dogs, shearing and wool classing). Robe has its own lobster fleet, and offers visitors a variety of grand fishing spots, on the beach, in the harbour or in a number of coastal lakes.

Tiny Beachport offers a Little Penguin rookery, excellent windsurfing on Lake George, great fishing and a range of Aboriginal associations. Millicent has an award-winning museum, owned by the National Trust. Millicent is the access point for Canunda National Park, which is the place to see huge sand dunes, wombats, emus and a great variety of water-loving birds, including the fish-catching Osprey (*left*). At the bottom of the south-east coast, Port MacDonnell has its own lobster fleet, mementos of Adam Lindsay Gordon and a Maritime Museum. Cave divers can find adventure at nearby Ewens Ponds and Picaninnie Ponds.

69

CENTRAL & WESTERN SOUTH AUSTRALIA

The driest State of the Commonwealth, South Australia encompasses huge desert areas. However, these vast spaces contain scenic spectaculars such as the astounding Flinders Ranges, with their daily shifts in colour and their springtime mantle of flowers. There are also ruins and ghost towns, memorials to failed farming hopes and too-hopeful mining ventures. A trustworthy vehicle, reserves of water, fuel and food and a love of adventure will reap many rewards here.

This camel's forebears were used by Afghans to transport goods.

THE FLINDERS RANGES

Famed for the colour-changes that sweep across them as the sun crosses the sky, the Flinders Ranges stretch for 400 km from Crystal Brook north to the edge of the Strzelecki Desert. They are reached via the towns of Port Augusta, Quorn and Hawker. Mount Remarkable National Park, in the southern Flinders Ranges, can be entered from Wilmington, and contains dramatic mountain vistas and some great bushwalks, including part of the Heysen Trail. Flinders Ranges National Park is in the central region, and offers magnificent scenery, including Wilpena Pound, and a wealth of wildlife, such as the Euro (below). Gammon Ranges National Park, to the north, is a rugged, wild area with some challenging walks. Its roads are best tackled in a 4WD vehicle (above).

Wilpena Pound, a vast natural amphitheatre, can be entered only through one narrow gorge.

RECORDS ON THE ROCKS

Aboriginal people have lived in the Flinders Ranges area for many thousands of years. The area was crossed by trade routes and contains many rock carvings and sites of significance to Aborigines. These should be treated with respect.

The Pichi Richi Railway gives a ride into the past.

HISTORY ON RAILS

Steam train buffs will enjoy visiting Quorn, about 50 km north-east of Port Augusta, en route to the Flinders Ranges. The Pichi Richi Railway, which uses historic rolling stock, runs from Quorn to Woolshed Pass, and the town's railway workshop displays many gems from the age of steam.

Aboriginal carvings in a dry creek bed in the Flinders Ranges.

Sheep are grazed on South Australia's low-rainfall areas.

The north of South Australia contains vast deserts.

Cliffs at Cape Carnot, south-east of Port Lincoln.

THE OUTBACK

South Australia's outback, which stretches from the head of Spencer Gulf to the borders of the Northern Territory and Queensland, and dips to the Nullarbor Plain in the far west, includes about 80% of the State. It has low rainfall, little surface water, and only about 1% of the State's population lives here. It is best to explore any part of the outback in cooler weather, and remember the stretches between refuelling points are sometimes lengthy. Many places, such as the rocket-launching town of Woomera, 490 km north-west of Adelaide, have interesting associations. Andamooka (600 km north of Adelaide) and Coober Pedy (845 km from Adelaide) are opal-mining towns with an underground lifestyle.

THE SCENIC WEST COAST

The Eyre Peninsula and the west coast offer fantastic seafood, marvellous coastal scenery, ocean dives (protected by a cage) to observe White Pointer Sharks, surfing, whale-watching and plenty of other activities. The steel town of Whyalla, gateway to the peninsula, has safe beaches and a Maritime Museum. Port Lincoln is the base for visits to Dangerous Reef, haunt of the great white shark, and is the place for magnificent seafood meals (it holds a Tunarama Festival each January). It is also a good jumping-off point to visit picturesque Lincoln and Coffin Bay National Parks. Further west, Ceduna is the last major town before the Nullarbor Plain. It offers fishing, boating, swimming, and a chance to prepare for the Nullarbor trek.

One of Coffin Bay National Park's unspoiled beaches.

WESTWARD ACROSS THE NULLARBOR

Bluebush on the Nullarbor Plain.

Highway 1 runs across the Nullarbor.

"Nullarbor" means "no trees", and much of the Nullarbor Plain is dotted with drought-tolerant shrubs such as saltbush and bluebush. It is home to many creatures, including the rare Southern Hairy-nosed Wombat, and has an extensive underground cave network. Between June and October, Head of Bight, which is Aboriginal land, is a good place to observe breeding Southern Right Whales.

Whale-watching.

Cliffs at Head of Bight are vantage points for whale-watchers.

Western Australia

INDIAN OCEAN

TIMOR SEA

Napier Broome Bay
Cape Bougainville
Cape Londonderry
Cape Ruthieres
Admiralty Gulf
Cape Voltaire
Kalumburu
Bigge Island
Joseph Bonaparte Gulf
Bonaparte Archipelago
Oombulgurri
Wyndham
Brunswick Bay
Augustus Island
Hall Point
Mt Hann 779 m
Kununurra
Collier Bay
Caroline Range
Buccaneer Archipelago
Cape Leveque
Lombadina
Beagle Bay
King Sound
Derby
Meda
Mt Hart 667 m
Mt Ord 947 m
Lake Argyle
Mt Wells 983 m
Bungle Bungle Range
Ord
Cape Baskerville
Dampier Land
"Kimberley Downs"
KIMBERLEY
Mt Laptz 645 m
Broome
"Udialla"
Fitzroy
River
Fitzroy Crossing
Great Antrim Plateau
Gantheaume Point
Roebuck Bay
Halls Creek
Cape Latouche Treville
Cape Bossut
"Christmas Creek"
Ck
Canning Basin
TANAMI DESERT
De Grey
River
North West Shelf
Port Hedland
Shay Gap
GREAT SANDY DESERT
Lake Gregory
NORTHERN TERRITORY
Monte Bello Islands
Point Samson
"Muccan"
Barrow Island
Dampier
Karratha
Marble Bar
Lake Waukarlycarly
Lake White
Lake Willis
Exmouth Gulf
Onslow
"Millstream"
Telfer
Lake Mackay
North West Cape
Exmouth
Pannawonica
Hamersley Range
Wittenoom
River
Nullagine
Lake Dora
Lake Auld
Percival Lakes
Learmonth
Tom Price
Mt Bruce 1235 m
Chabjuwardoo Bay
Mt Meharry 1253 m
Opthalmia Range
Paraburdoo
Mt Gascoyne 790 m
Mt Newman 1057 m
Newman
Jiggalong
Lake Disappointment
Lake MacDonald
Cape Farquhar
Kennedy Range
Barlee Range
"Bulloo Downs"
WESTERN AUSTRALIA
Petermann
Lyons
Carnarvon Range
GIBSON DESERT
Mt Augustus 1105 m
Mt Egerton 994 m
Ranges
Kaltukatjara
Gascoyne Junction
Gascoyne
"Giles Meteorological Station"
Bernier Island
Lake MacLeod
"Dalgety Downs"
Robinson Range
Mt Deering 1219 m
Dorre Island
Carnarvon
R
"Coordewandy"
Mt Fraser 770 m
Warburton Range
Cape Inscription
Dirk Hartog Island
Shark Bay
Mt Gould 710 m
Glengarry Range
Warburton
Mt Squires 704 m
Blackstone Range
Mt Aloysius 982 m
Peron Pen
Wooramel
Karalundi
Ernest
Mt Hale 697 m
Steep Point
Denham
Murchison
Meekatharra
Lake Carnegie
Giles Range
Weld Range
Cue
Lake Austin
Wiluna
Lake Wells
Mt Bryan 599 m
Kalbarri
Gantheaume Bay
Mount Magnet
Sandstone
GREAT VICTORIA DESERT
Houtman Abrolhos
Yalgoo
Rason Lake
Geraldton
Greenough
R
Lake Barlee
Leonora
Laverton
Gwalia
Lake Carey
Morawa
Mt Singleton 678 m
Lake Ballard
Dongara
Lake Minigwal
Menzies
Lake Moore
Mt Jackson 617 m
NULLARBOR PLAIN
Dalwallinu
Kalannie
Bonnie Rock
Moora
Miling
Koolyanobbing
Kalgoorlie
Karonie
Forrest
Lancelin
Bullfinch
Coolgardie
Boulder
Kitchener
Rawlinna
Loongana
Cook
Southern Cross
Kambalda
Wanneroo
Northam
Merredin
Widgiemooltha
Lake Lefroy
Perth
Kellerberrin
Lake Cowan
Hampton Tableland
Rottnest Island
York
Skeleton Rock 458 m
Symons Hill 394 m
Fremantle
Lake Johnston
Kwinana
Brookton
Hyden
Norseman
Rockingham
Jarrahdale
Lake Dundas
Eucla
Mandurah
Pinjarra
Kondinin
Boddington
Narrogin
Newdegate
Great Australian Bight
Harvey
Collie
Wagin
Point Culver
Bunbury
Donnybrook
Nyabing
Ravensthorpe
Geographe Bay
Cape Naturaliste
Busselton
Katanning
Point Malcolm
Margaret River
Kojonup
Gnowangerup
Hopetoun
Bridgetown
Esperance
Augusta
Manjimup
Bluff Knoll 1096 m
Point Hood
Cape Leeuwin
Pemberton
Mount Barker
Bremer Bay
Cape Knob
Flinders Bay
Northcliffe
Denmark
Esperance Bay
Archipelago of the Recherche
Point D'Entrecasteaux
Walpole
Albany
Point Nuyts
West Cape Howe
King George Sound

SOUTH AUSTRALIA

0   150   300 km

115° E   120° E   125° E   130° E

15° S
20° S
25° S
30° S
35° S

72

Western Australia is the largest Australian State. Occupying one-third of the continent, it has around 12 500 km of coastline. A lifetime could be spent touring this great State, with its wide variety of landscapes and wide range of climates. If time is limited, there are plenty of attractions in the compact south-west corner, and plans to be made for the next visit to "the golden West".

Western Australia's capital, Perth, is gifted with a wonderful Mediterranean climate, magnificent beaches, the Swan River and, in spring, beautiful wildflowers. Nearby, the historic port of Fremantle is the access point for the popular holiday island of Rottnest. The south-west of the State offers fine wines, rugged coastal scenery and towering forests. The south coast has some of the world's finest remaining pristine beaches. North of Perth are wildflower-embroidered sandplains, the charms of Kalbarri National Park and the remarkable dolphins of Shark Bay. Further north still are the scenic splendours of the Hamersley Ranges and the rugged wilderness and wide plains of the Kimberley.

WESTERN AUSTRALIA

PAGES 72–89

PERTH & SURROUNDS

The Black Swan is one of the emblems of Western Australia.

PERTH

The paddlewheeler *Decoy* against the city skyline.

Perth seen at dusk from Kings Park.

Perth is a beautiful city with a charm all its own. Basking on the banks of the broad Swan River in the relatively warm winters and hot summers of a Mediterranean climate, the capital of Western Australia is a memorable place to visit. Perth, and its sister-port, Fremantle, are more than 2000 km distant from Adelaide. Their residents are remarkably self-sufficient in matters of art, cuisine and culture: the depth of local talent is showcased in the Festival of Perth held each February–March.

SWAN CITY

In 1827, the British Government agreed to a settlement on the Swan River, hoping to forestall French claims to Australia's west coast. A syndicate was formed to establish settlers on the Swan River and in 1829 Captain Fremantle claimed the area and Perth was established under Governor James Stirling. By 1844 the colony was

languishing and the settlers asked for convicts. The first arrived in 1850 and transportation did not stop until 1868, when the colony was doing well. The gold rushes of the 1890s provided Perth with impetus for growth and some fine buildings. In the final quarter of the twentieth century, mining again provided wealth to transform Perth into the charming city it is today.

A view of Perth showing Kings Park, the Narrows Interchange and Narrows Bridge, and the Swan River.

THE GLORIOUS SWAN RIVER

The Swan River curves through the centre of Perth. An efficient bus service provides public transport to the parks, playing fields, walking and cycling tracks that border the river. Families swim at the sandy beaches, and picnic or barbecue in parklands shaded by spreading gums and peppermint trees. There are also some great fishing spots along the Swan.

The more daring can enjoy sailing a private or hire craft (*left*) or jetskiing (*far left*), or soaring across Perth Water in a hang-glider towed off the river by a powerboat. Cruise vessels leave from the Barrack St Jetty for trips to the wineries of the Upper Swan or to Fremantle. The tidal Swan is Perth's playground, and any visit to the city should include a stroll around the lakes at the Narrows Interchange and a voyage upon the river's blue expanse.

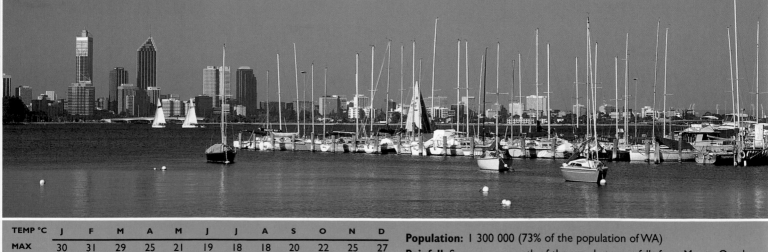

TEMP °C	J	F	M	A	M	J	J	A	S	O	N	D
MAX	30	31	29	25	21	19	18	18	20	22	25	27
MIN	18	19	17	14	12	10	9	9	10	12	14	17

Population: 1 300 000 (73% of the population of WA)
Rainfall: Some every month of the year, but most falls from May to October.

KINGS PARK

Sufficient time to investigate the treasures of Kings Park is an absolute imperative on any visit to Perth. This unique green area on the heights of Mt Eliza overlooking Perth Water encompasses 4 sq km, and includes large expanses of bushland traversed by paths and tracks. The park also harbours lawns, lakes, monuments and a 17 ha Botanic Gardens where massed displays of West Australian wildflowers and a number of theme gardens can be enjoyed. A Wildflower Display held each September exhibits flora from all over the State. There's a restaurant and floral clock (*above right*), a café and souvenir shops and some fine vantage points from which to take panoramic photographs of Perth and the Swan River. The tram shown below right travels between the park, the city and Burswood Casino.

WHERE IS IT?

1	Parliament House	11	Government House
2	Hay St	12	Supreme Court
3	Entertainment Centre	13	The Esplanade
4	Northbridge	14	Burswood Casino
5	Railway Station	15	WA Cricket Ground
6	WA Art Gallery	16	The Causeway
7	Barracks Arch	17	Swan River
8	St Georges Tce	18	Barrack St Jetty
9	Hay St Mall	19	Narrows Interchange
10	City Busport		

The facade of London Court in Hay St Mall.

IN THE 'BURBS

Perth city is compact and well laid out. It is remarkably easy to travel around city and suburbs by car, or on a city bus, or on the trains that connect the city to Fremantle, Armadale, Midland and the northern centre of Joondalup. Cruises from Barrack St Jetty visit Fremantle and scenic spots on the Swan River. Some of Perth's most interesting attractions are to be found in the suburbs. Besides plenty of places to eat, there are the fascinating markets in the Subiaco Pavilion and at outer suburbs such as Wanneroo. The Old Mill and the popular Zoological Gardens are in South Perth. The Scitech Discovery Centre in West Perth has many hands-on exhibits, and those interested in Aboriginal art should not miss the Berndt Museum of Anthropology at the University of Western Australia at Crawley. Burswood Casino (below) is on an island in the Swan River east of the city centre.

Perth has a fine sense of its history and many nineteenth-century buildings, such as the Old Courthouse (1836), the Cloisters (1858), Old Perth Boys School (1854) and the Barracks Arch (1863) can be seen on a Heritage day-tour of the city. The broad arrows beside the clock of the Town Hall (*inset below*) are said to have been deliberately inserted by the convicts who built it in the late 1860s. The Perth Mint, further east on Hay Street, became operative in 1899 after huge gold finds at Coolgardie and Kalgoorlie. It is open to the public.

Forrest Place is one of Perth's most popular city spaces.

A CITY TO DINE OUT IN

Perth is a marvellous place in which to eat out. It has a seemingly endless supply of fresh local produce, and its multicultural population has encouraged the growth of restaurants featuring a wide range of tasty ethnic cuisines. Northbridge, just over the Horseshoe Bridge from the city centre, and the suburbs of Subiaco and Leederville are particularly well-endowed with pleasant places to dine in style.

ARTS, CRAFTS AND THEATRES

Isolation has fostered Perth's vigorous cultural life. The WA Art Gallery, adjacent to the metropolitan railway station, is noted for its collections and there are many art and craft galleries in city and suburbs. Theatre is vigorous in Perth – His Majesty's and the Playhouse in the city, and the Regal in Subiaco, all stage local and touring hits. The Entertainment Centre and the Concert Hall stage concerts and productions at all levels.

Hay St Mall, the entrance to London Court and the Town Hall.

The ornate facade of His Majesty's Theatre.

Perth's great climate means lots of outdoor eateries.

The Art Gallery is near the Museum and the railway station.

VINEYARDS OF THE SWAN

Learning about grapes on a vineyard at Upper Swan.

The church gate shown below marks the furthest point reached by Captain Stirling in 1827, when he travelled up the Swan River valley searching for better soils than existed on the coastal plain. Today a Heritage trail retraces Stirling's steps, and the fertile river flats he explored are the sites for numerous wineries. Enter the wine country through the historic town of Guildford, and tour the Swan, Henley Brook and Upper Swan regions for wines, craft and art galleries, antiques and warm hospitality.

THE DARLING RANGE

The Darling Range, the south-western edge of a state-wide plateau, is full of enjoyable places. At Armadale, 40 minutes from Perth, Pioneer World gives insight into life in the 1800s. Another charming town, Kalamunda is near the lovely Araluen gardens. Mundaring Weir, Lake Leschenaultia and John Forrest National Park are places to walk, swim and picnic. The Avon River is popular with canoeists, and Northam, York, Toodyay and Beverley are towns with historic and many other attractions.

Peaceful pastures in the Darling Range.

Pioneer cart wheel and Twenty-eight Ringneck Parrot.

Wildflowers in John Forrest National Park.

PERTH'S BEACHES

Within easy driving distance of Perth there is a beach to suit every possible requirement. A chain of surf beaches, usually patrolled by surf lifesavers (*below*), stretches from Port Beach, just north of Fremantle, to Sorrento. Cottesloe, Scarborough and City Beaches are excellent and well-patrolled family beaches. Swanbourne, just up the coast from North Cottesloe, is a nude bathing beach. Hillarys Boat Harbour, just north of Sorrento Beach, has the attraction of Underwater World, whose underwater tunnel aquarium is home to over 200 species of marine animals, including stingrays and sharks. Whale-watching expeditions set out from Hillarys when Humpback Whales are swimming past.

City Beach.

The beach at Hillarys Boat Harbour, Sorrento.

Cottesloe is a safe family beach.

Above & below: Fremantle's café society.

DINING DELIGHTS

Fremantle has an infinite variety of great places to eat. Marvellous seafood can be bought over the counter, or savoured in restaurants, around the Fishing Boat Harbour and on the Esplanade. On Market Street, which becomes South Terrace, there are many popular coffee shops and bistros. East Fremantle's George St has a group of good restaurants, and while Fremantle is noted for great Italian food the cuisines of other nations can be found with little effort, and the Fremantle Markets are a good place to start.

Fremantle, at the mouth of the Swan River, has a population of around 25 000 and an identity quite separate from that of Perth, 19 km away. The port city is a centre for artists and craftworkers, and restoration of its limestone public buildings and workers' houses has preserved its nineteenth-century appeal. The Port of Fremantle, which owes its fine harbour to turn-of-the-century engineering genius Charles Yelverton O'Connor, is modern and efficient. Fishing Boat Harbour has a Mediterranean air, while Success Harbour is a safe anchorage.

Fremantle Museum was built in the 1860s as a lunatic asylum and is now a well-known cultural and artistic centre.

The Round House was convict-built as a gaol in 1831. The tunnel beneath was dug in 1837 to connect beach and town.

A Fremantle street vendor and her colourful wares.

A Fremantle Tram, which tours the city, can be boarded outside the Town Hall, a building that dates from 1887.

WHERE IS IT?

The Underwater Explorer has windows below the waterline.

Ospreys nest on Rottnest.

Fun on the beach.

Holiday cottages, Thomson Bay.

Cyclists and lighthouse.

One of Australia's most favoured holiday destinations, Rottnest is a low island 11 km long and 5 km wide lying 19 km off the coast from Fremantle. It was named "Rats' Nest" by Dutch Captain de Vlamingh in 1696 after he misidentified the small wallabies, the Quokkas (*below*), common on the island. Used from 1838 to 1903 as a prison for Aborigines, Rottnest is now one of Australia's most popular holiday destinations. Access is by air, or by ferry or jetcat from Fremantle. There is plenty to do, including swimming, fishing, cruising in a glass-bottomed boat, meeting Quokkas, bird-watching on the salt lakes and shore (the fish-eating Ospreys are a highlight), diving, eating and simply relaxing in the cottages at Thomson Bay settlement (*left*). Rottnest is almost car-free, and bicycles are easily hired and universally used.

THE SOUTH-WEST CORNER

The south-west corner of Western Australia is well-favoured climatically, with plentiful winter rains and pleasant, warm summers. The coastline is well provided with rugged granite headlands (*left*), secluded beaches and heathlands that, in springtime, are covered with flowers. Bunbury, a major port, has a beach visited by friendly Bottlenose Dolphins. Inland are magnificent forests, including the giant Karris and Red Tingles, and a rural landscape with rolling hills dotted with grazing sheep, orchards of apples, pears and other fruits, and some classic wineries.

Surfers ride the rolling breakers on the south-west coast.

AMONGST THE TALL TREES

The towering Karri and Red Tingle are amongst the world's tallest trees. Stands of Karri may be seen near Margaret River, but Manjimup (307 km south of Perth) and Pemberton (335 km) are the best places to view the giants. At Pemberton, the daring may climb the Gloucester Tree to a fire lookout 60 m above the ground. Warren, Shannon and Beedelup National Parks are other forest sanctuaries: Warren National Park, near Pemberton, boasts a Karri 69 m tall.

MARGARET RIVER

There are few towns that offer so many attractions for families and adventurers as Margaret River. Some 280 km from Perth, it is famous for its world-class wines, its marvellous surf beaches, its scenic surroundings, both coastal and on the Margaret River, and its resident artists and craftspeople. Twenty-one km to the south-west is Mammoth Cave, famous for its fossils. The wineries and restaurants of Margaret River cooperate to provide gourmet delights, including marron (freshwater crayfish), trout and luscious local cheeses.

Sculpture decorates the Rose Hotel roundabout, Bunbury.

COASTAL SPLENDOUR

South of Perth, Bunbury and Busselton are popular coastal holiday towns. At Busselton, the coastline plunges westwards, then turns south again at Cape Naturaliste. Between here and Cape Leeuwin, the long swells from Africa and the westerly winds have shaped magnificent coastal scenery. In the hinterland are rivers, caves, forests, birdlife and wildflowers in spring and summer.

Driving through the tall trees of Shannon National Park.

The lookout at Sugarloaf Rock, just south of Cape Naturaliste, is a favourite place for photographers and birdwatchers.

A pristine beach in William Bay National Park, between the towns of Walpole and Denmark.

Granite headlands defy the sea near Albany.

THE GREAT SOUTHERN DISTRICT

The area from Cape Leeuwin to Albany is worth a leisurely visit, for it includes some wonderful country to admire and explore. Two inlets are bordered by Walpole-Nornalup National Park, which is famed for its lovely beaches and for the Valley of the Giants, a stand of massive Karri and Red Tingle trees. The Nuyts Wilderness, near Walpole, offers a walking track through forests and coastal heathland. The Bibbulmun Track, a walking trail that begins at Kalamunda near Perth, ends 530 km later at Walpole. In springtime, wildflowers (*above right*) cover the heathlands in colour.

ALBANY AND ITS SURROUNDS

In 1826, Albany was settled because of fears that the French would claim the south-west. Later, it became a whaling port. Today Albany is a popular holiday centre, whose historic attractions include Strawberry Hill Farm (dating to 1827), the Residency Museum, and the Princess Royal Fortress. South of Albany is Torndirrup National Park, which contains some stunning scenery, including the spectacular Gap, Natural Bridge and the Blowholes. East of Albany in Waychinicup National Park, Whaleworld Museum at the now defunct Cheyne Beach Whaling Station records the whaling industry's past.

Albany Town Hall and Princess Royal Harbour.

The Gap, an awesome chasm in Torndirrup National Park.

The Salmon Holes, one of the many beautiful coves on the south coast near Albany.

Albany's supercilious Dog Rock.

The rocky coast of Cape Le Grand NP.

Two Peoples Bay.

A visit to the south coast of Western Australia would be incomplete without seeing the Porongurup and Stirling Ranges, each making up a national park and offering many challenges to bushwalkers and rock-climbers. The Porongurups are small in extent, but their scenic impact is high and their diverse vegetation includes both wildflowers and Karri trees. The Stirling Range is a line of peaks, with Bluff Knoll rising to 1073 m. Wildflower enthusiasts revel in this park's spring display, when nearly all the area's 1500 species of plants seem to be in bloom.

Wildflowers cover the south coast plains in springtime.

The brooding profile of the Stirling Range at dawn, before the sun has burned the mist from the valleys.

REDISCOVERED!

The coastal heathlands east of Albany lure birdwatchers from all over the world to try to catch a glimpse of a drab-plumaged but loud-voiced, ground-living bird. The Noisy Scrub-bird had not been sighted since 1889 and was thought to be extinct when rediscovered on the site of a proposed township at Two Peoples Bay in 1961. The area was proclaimed a reserve and today the Noisy Scrub-bird seems secure, if the heathlands remain unravaged by fire.

The Quokka, best-known from Rottnest Island, also lives in this habitat. In 1994, when two researchers were trapping Quokkas at Two Peoples Bay, they realised with amazement that they had caught a Gilbert's Potoroo (*above right*), a small relative of the kangaroos, which had not been sighted in WA for 115 years.

The coastal heaths and the thickly-vegetated gullies of Western Australia's south coast are home to a wealth of small mammals and birds, and no nature-lover should miss the opportunity to wander, binoculars at the ready.

FROM ALBANY TO ESPERANCE

It is 476 km from Albany to the port of Esperance, which lies directly south of the gold and nickel fields of Norseman and Kalgoorlie. Bremer Bay is 80 km along the coast from the old whaling station at Cheyne Beach. It is a good base for watching Southern Right Whales, which give birth in coves in the area and may be seen very close inshore. Further east, Hopetoun is an access point for Fitzgerald River National Park, which UNESCO has classified as a World Biosphere Reserve. This park is notable for its unspoiled coastal scenery, and for the great variety of its wildflowers and wildlife. Two of its plants, the Royal Hakea and the Qualup Bell, are unique.

Esperance, once the port for the goldfields and 720 km from Perth, is today the centre for a busy pastoral industry and a popular summer resort. Cruises around the 105 small offshore islands of the Archipelago of the Recherche land on Woody Island. About 50 km east of Esperance is scenic Cape Le Grand National Park, popular with bushwalkers and nature-lovers.

Headland in Fitzgerald River National Park, near Hopetoun.

Silver sand dunes in Cape Le Grand National Park.

A bay in Cape Arid National Park, east of Esperance.

Footsteps on the dunes of Eucla National Park.

THE GOLDFIELDS

Kalgoorlie.

Goldfields landscape.

Gold was discovered in 1892 at Coolgardie (by 1898 Coolgardie had a population of 15 000) and later at Kalgoorlie: many smaller strikes followed. A tour of the Goldfields is memorable for ghost towns, grandiose ruins, the flourishing city of Kalgoorlie and, after rain, deserts vivid with flowers.

FROM ESPERANCE TO EUCLA

Cape Arid National Park lies on the edge of the Nullarbor Plain and borders the Great Australian Bight. It is a wonderful getaway for those interested in walking, fishing, camping and 4WD expeditions. Travellers in such isolated areas should be completely self-sufficient (even firewood is scarce) and make sure their vehicle is reliable. Those swimming or diving in the sea should be wary of sharks where seals are common.

Highway 1 goes north from Esperance to Norseman, then turns east for the long haul across the Nullarbor Plain then over the South Australian border. Along the way, it is worth looking (very carefully) at the caves that honeycomb parts of the Plain; at Eyre Bird Observatory in Nuytsland Nature Reserve on the coast south of Cocklebiddy; and at the magnificent sand dunes around Eucla that are gradually engulfing the old telegraph station there.

THE WHEATBELT

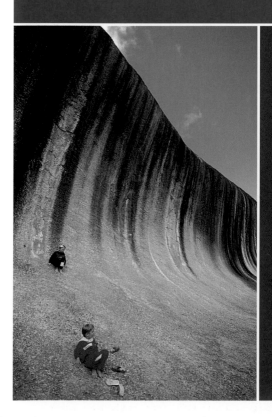

Wheat and wool are produced in the region extending east from the forests of the Darling Range until rainfall becomes too low and irregular. Often in the "wheatbelt" the native vegetation has been reduced to road verges, but dry-country eucalypts such as the mallees (*top right*) continue to provide shade and spring flowers. Dryandra State Forest, in the southern Wheatbelt, is a refuge for the beautiful, and endangered, Numbat and other mammals. The rock outcrops, or tors, of the Wheatbelt stand defiantly in the middle of paddocks. Wave Rock (*left*), near Hyden, 350 km east of Perth, is a crest of rock 100 m long and 15 m high, streaked with pigment deposited by rain runoff.

FROM PERTH TO SHARK BAY

The coastal plains north of Perth are at their best with wildflowers from July to October. However, at any time of the year it is exhilarating to travel the long highway that links the Swan River with Shark Bay World Heritage and Marine Park. Past Yanchep, with its caves, is Nambung National Park with its famous Pinnacles. Further north are the sun-drenched coastal towns (heaven on earth for people who fish and eat fish) of Port Denison and Geraldton. The dramatic red gorges of Kalbarri National Park are a prelude to the dolphins of Monkey Mia.

Everlasting daisies, common on the sandplains.

SANDPLAINS STORY

The sandplains of Western Australia's central coast are rich with life. Native vegetation has adapted to make the most of sandy soils that are poor in plant food and, in spring, kangaroo paws, banksias and many other flowering plants paint the landscape in rich colour.

Many animals, such as the Gould's Goanna (*below*), retreat into burrows during the hot summer, emerging in the cool evening to find food. There are even frogs that live most of their lives underground to breed after rain. The sandplain flowers attract birds and small native mammals that feed on nectar and on the insects that swarm to it.

TWO ROADS TO THE NORTH

While Highway 1 keeps near the coast on its northward exit from Perth, the Great Northern Highway runs more or less parallel to it further inland. After leaving the wine country of the Swan Valley it passes through New Norcia, where in 1846 Spanish Benedictine monks established a monastery (*right*). Today the order's farm produces wool and wheat and the monastery is well worth a visit to view its museum and an art gallery that houses priceless examples of religious art. A left turn at Mingenew, 150 km north on the Midlands Road, will bring travellers once more to Highway 1 at the historic town of Dongara, near Port Denison, a popular coastal resort.

WHERE NAVIGATORS DARED

The western coastline of Australia has a wealth of associations with early Dutch navigators. East India Company ships ran before strong westerly winds from the Cape of Good Hope across the Indian Ocean and sometimes sighted "New Holland". Dirk Hartog landed at Shark Bay in 1616, and, after exploring Rottnest, so did Willem de Vlamingh in 1697. The *Leeuwin* visited the southwest coast in 1622. In 1629, the wreck of the silver-laden *Batavia* on Houtmans Abrolhos led to a saga of mutiny, massacre and retribution. (The story is retold dramatically in Fremantle's Maritime Museum.) This wreck, and many others, continue to yield up secrets.

NAMBUNG NATIONAL PARK

The Pinnacles, which rise from the sands of Nambung National Park, are pillars of limestone that formed around the roots of long-vanished trees, then were uncovered by the wind. They rise up to 5 m from the sand in an area whose wildflower display is at its peak from August to October. Other local features are dunes, the Painted Desert and the Tombstones. Entry to the park is through the town of Cervantes, 257 km north of Perth: it is worth arriving early in the morning or late in the afternoon to catch the best light.

Nature's Window, a sandstone arch that frames a panorama of Kalbarri National Park.

WILDERNESS IN SANDSTONE

The town of Kalbarri stands at the mouth of the Murchison River, 660 km north of Perth. Kalbarri National Park protects 80 km of gorges carved into a plateau of red and white Tumblagooda sandstone by the Murchison. The park contains over 800 different flowering plants (*right*): Kalflora, in Kalbarri, offers information about them. Canoe-borne river explorers, wildlife enthusiasts, bushwalkers and birdwatchers will all enjoy the area.

SHARK BAY WILDERNESS

Exploring Shark Bay World Heritage and Marine Park is an eye-opening experience. The seemingly harsh landscape of the Peron Peninsula has become a sanctuary for rare mammals and birds, and the waters of Shark Bay shelter, among other sea creatures, Bottlenose Dolphins and the endangered Dugong. Stromatolites, domed formations that are modern representatives of the oldest known lifeforms, are found in Hamelin Pool.

The warm-toned earth of the Peron Peninsula.

The Zuytdorp Cliffs extend north from Kalbarri.

THE DOLPHINS OF MONKEY MIA

Shark Bay is 840 km north of Perth, and Monkey Mia (*left*) is a beach 26 km from the bayside town of Denham. Here Bottlenose Dolphins (*above*) come, usually in the morning, to pass some time with humans. Groups of visitors can fly in to an airstrip near Denham, and a hovercraft makes the trip south from Carnarvon in 90 minutes.

The slopes of Mt Augustus.

The vast spaces of the Pilbara region.

The north-west of Western Australia is an ancient region, whose rocks are amongst the oldest known on the surface of the planet. It is a place of stark and dramatic landscapes, with wide red plains studded with cushiony mounds of spinifex, interrupted by rocky outcrops and steep-sided buttes. Its plants and animals are as fascinating as the land itself. Many towns in the region, that provide bases for travellers, were established to service the mining and grazing industries.

NORTH-WEST TOWNS

Carnarvon, at the mouth of the Gascoyne River and a major tropical fruit growing centre, is 904 km north of Perth. The Gascoyne flows below ground in its lower reaches. At Carnarvon, bores bring up water to irrigate plantations. Carnarvon is the nearest town to Kennedy Range National Park. Gascoyne Junction, 174 km east, is the gateway to Mt Augustus National Park. Exmouth, on the north-east side of North West Cape, is the nearest town to Cape Range National Park and Ningaloo Marine Park. The closest centre to Karijini National Park is Tom Price, through Newman, on the Great Northern Highway, or Port Hedland can serve as a gateway to Karijini also.

NIGHT-HOWLERS

Australia's wild dog, the Dingo (right), may be seen near water anywhere in the north-west. A pack of Dingos consists of a breeding pair and their relatives. They combine to hunt and rear pups.

Rugged desert beauty in Kennedy Range National Park, east of Carnarvon.

MIGHTY MT AUGUSTUS

Gascoyne Junction, where the Lyons and Gascoyne Rivers meet, is 174 km east of Carnarvon. Those who wish to see the world's greatest rock will journey another 315 km to where Mt Augustus rises 1106 m above sea level. Mt Augustus is twice the size of Uluru, but seems less impressive than the central Australian monolith because of its stepped formation and the trees on its flanks. Its granite is estimated to be 1750 million years old, and to the Aboriginal people of the area it represents the body of a speared traveller named Burringurrah, after whom the national park is named.

A billabong on the Gascoyne River near Gascoyne Junction.

Mt Augustus is 490 km from Carnarvon, and a view such as this is well worth the long journey through the aridlands.

A magical oasis in Karijini National Park.

Karijini National Park lies in the heart of a massive iron-mining operation whose ore travels to the port of Dampier on trains 2 km long. The park offers memorable scenery, with gorges providing soothing, sometimes water-cooled, beauty within frames of hot red rock. Those who wish to track the southwards blossoming of Western Australia's wildflowers should begin in Karijini, and a quiet watcher at any waterhole will observe plenty of wildlife. Scenic Millstream-Chichester National Park is about 150 km south of Roebourne.

Weano Gorge.

Spinifex and Ghost Gums.

Iron ore trains.

A Whale Shark, huge but harmless to humans.

NINGALOO MARINE PARK

The 260 km stretch of Ningaloo Reef that forms Ningaloo Marine Park, on the seaward side of North West Cape, is a salt water wonderland. Nesting Green Turtles, migrating Humpback Whales, awesome Whale Sharks and huge Manta Rays can be seen here at various times of the year. This is a marvellous coral reef, close to shore and with an enormous diversity of lifeforms. Exmouth has good dive facilities.

MARBLE BAR

Marble Bar, south-east of Port Hedland, was so-named because of an outcrop of red jasper across the Coongan River near the town site. Gold was discovered here in 1890, but today visitors are interested in the "marble" bar, in the wildflowers of early spring and in visiting Doolena Gorge, 70 km from town. Very hot in summer, the region is pleasantly sunny in winter.

Marble Bar's "marble bar" is really jasper.

Termite mounds stand amidst spinifex clumps.

TERMITES AND SPINIFEX

The brick-hard, soil-coloured mounds that dot northern Australia are the work of tiny, blind insects called termites. The mounds, with their extensive underground tunnels, harbour the egg-laying queen termite, the soldiers and countless workers that leave the nest at night to harvest spinifex or other plant material as food and building material.

Ancient weathered rock of the Kimberley.

Boab trees silhouetted against a Kimberley dawn.

Broome, just over 600 km from Port Hedland, is the south-western gateway to the fabulous Kimberley Division. In many Kimberley fastnesses, nature rules and the impact of humans seems minimal. It is easy to become entranced by the majesty of the ranges, the spaciousness of the plains studded with termite mounds and Boab trees, and the mystery of the impenetrable wilderness that safeguards the northern coastlands. Those who visit the Kimberley will always long to return.

THE PEARLING DAYS

In the 1800s, the demand for pearl shell to be cut into mother-of-pearl buttons was great, and by the early 1900s there were around 400 pearling luggers working out of the port of Broome. The perils of the sea were great and today the cemetery at Broome displays the tombstones of many divers, a fair number of whom were Japanese. Gradually demand for pearl shell declined and in the mid-1900s plastic buttons replaced pearly ones.

Broome today has a multicultural population, and is popular as a sunny winter resort. Holiday-makers can walk the sands of Cable Beach (or ride a camel), marvel at dinosaur footprints and cultured pearls, and remember the days of old, when brave divers risked their lives to bring up shell and Broome was the pearling capital of the world.

Inset above: The Whistling Kite, a common bird of prey in the Kimberley.

LAND UNDER THE MONSOON

The Kimberley lies under the influence of the monsoons, which bring cyclonic rain during the hot summer Wet, then retreat to leave the land pleasantly warm but dry during winter. Visit in winter for best climatic conditions, but be aware that after the "build-up" of October and November heavy rain will change the land to green and set birds singing and breeding. Fitzroy Crossing, 260 km inland from Derby on the Northern Highway, is near Geikie Gorge National Park, where coloured cliffs are reflected in still water that harbours wildlife including Freshwater Crocodiles. North of the Derby–Fitzroy Crossing road is Windjana Gorge National Park, where the Lennard River has carved gorges up to 90 m deep through an ancient reef. At nearby Tunnel Creek National Park, a tunnel 750 m long and up to 15 m wide penetrates the Napier Range.

Windjana Gorge, in Jundumurra country.

HERO OF THE RESISTANCE

Jundumurra, or Pigeon, was a leader of the Aboriginal resistance to European settlement in the Kimberley. He took refuge in the Napier Range and was eventually killed in Tunnel Creek. There is a Pigeon Heritage Trail, which can be traced from either Broome or Derby.

Memorials to the pearling days.

TEMP °C	J	F	M	A	M	J	J	A	S	O	N	D
MAX	36	35	35	35	33	31	30	32	35	36	37	37
MIN	26	26	25	22	19	16	14	16	20	23	25	26

Rainfall: Most falls between December and March.

Photo above: Droving cattle across a West Kimberley plain.

Above: Some climatic data for the town of Derby.

The stunning and isolated country around the Prince Regent River is UNESCO-classed as a World Biosphere Reserve.

Bell Gorge, in King Leopold Range National Park.

Walcott Inlet extends 30 km inland from Collier Bay. No roads penetrate this northern wilderness.

NORTH AND EAST KIMBERLEY

Only the determined traveller will manage to see areas of the north Kimberley, such as Drysdale River National Park and the Prince Regent Nature Reserve. These are rugged wilderness areas, difficult of access and with no amenities. Spectacular scenery and the chance of discovering species new to science are rewards for those lucky enough to get to these places.

Kununurra, 36 km from the Northern Territory border on Highway 1, was founded in the 1960s. From Kununurra it is possible to fish or cruise on nearby Lake Argyle, or to take a guided tour of the Argyle Diamond Mine, which produces around 35% of the world's diamonds. Mirima National Park, near Kununurra, offers panoramic views from the summit of a sandstone range.

Kimberley waterways are home to harmless Freshwater Crocodiles (*above*). Rivers flowing to the sea harbour the dangerous Saltwater Crocodile.

Until quite recently, Purnululu, a range of reddish rock domes striped green-black with lichen, five hours' drive from Kununurra, was comparatively unknown. Today it is a national park, accessible by four-wheel-drive vehicles (the fragile domes should not be climbed). It can also be viewed from a helicopter or light plane.

Where Aboriginal art is seen, it should be respected.

A dry riverbed winds through the domes of Purnululu National Park, 305 km from Kununurra.

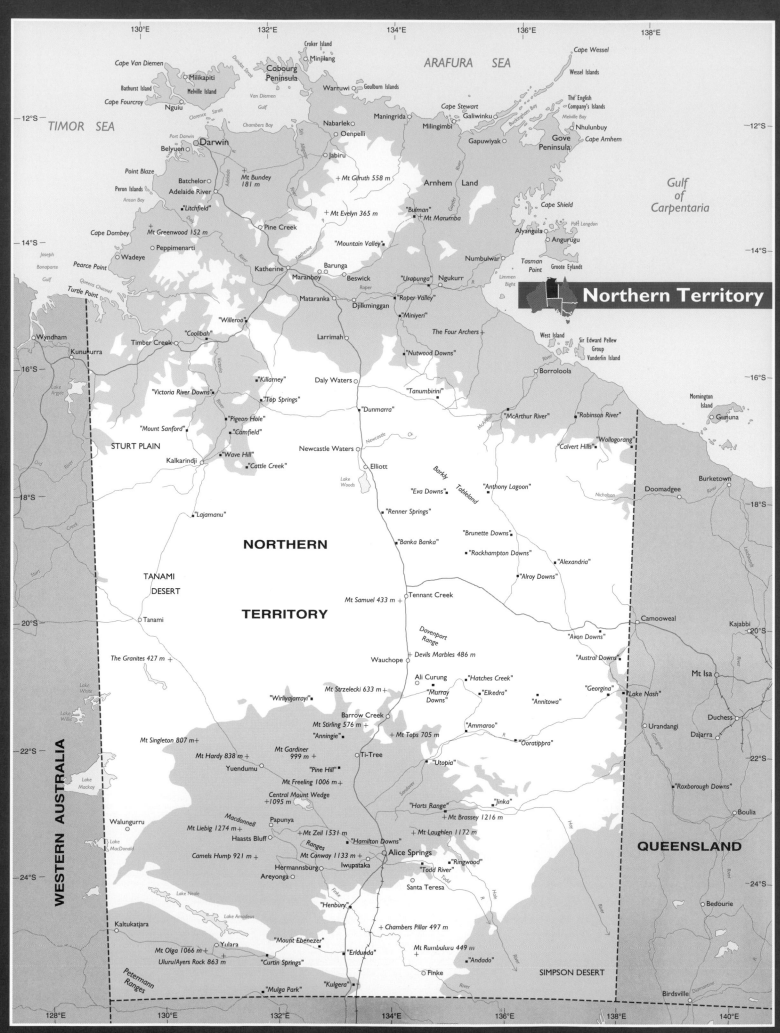

Northern Territory

The Northern Territory is vast and its magic places are many. A few are well documented – someone who has never been to the Territory can still have a mental picture of Uluṟu rising in majesty from the surrounding desert, or of a waterfall thundering over sandstone cliffs in Kakadu National Park. However, the real thing is awe-inspiring, and an unforgettable experience.

NORTHERN TERRITORY

PAGES 90–101

In this land of legends, the reflections that reach the outside world are often less remarkable than their originals. It is a place of dramatic contrasts. The Top End in the summer Wet is different from the same country in the Dry. The monsoon wetlands of the tropical north could be halfway around the world from the vast aridlands of the Red Centre.

Darwin, Australia's most isolated capital city, is the administrative centre of the Northern Territory. Its friendly people, a rich mix of races, and its remoteness give Darwin an exotic, somewhat eccentric character.

The Northern Territory is a place of natural wonders and rich human experiences, where in many places the Aboriginal people who have lived there for many tens of thousands of years are still looking after their country.

DARWIN & SURROUNDS

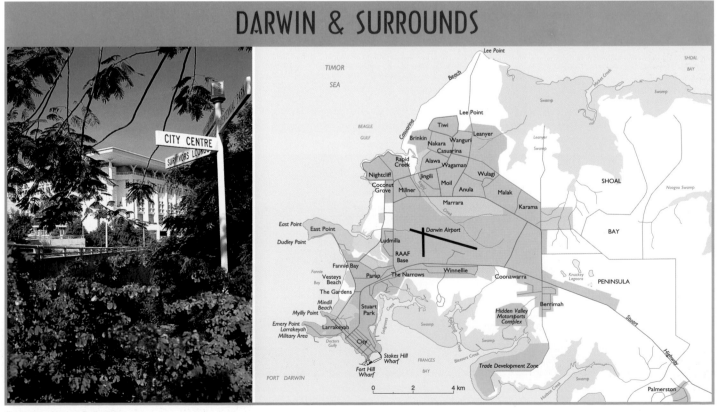

Parliament House, Darwin.

Darwin survived the 64 air-raids of World War II only to be flattened by Cyclone Tracy on Christmas Day, 1974. The rebuilt Darwin is spacious and bright with colourful tropical gardens. Its new buildings are constructed to make the most of the warm climate and to weather any future cyclones. Torrential summer rains do not slow the pace of life in the city, though many people prefer the less humid months of May to September. Today's Darwin is a centre of government and of competitive, modern business and commerce. It is a vigorous, enjoyable, modern city, though many memories of the pioneer days can be found by those who look for them.

An elegant survivor of war and cyclone.

NORTHERNMOST CITY

The Aboriginal people have lived in the Top End of the Northern Territory for more than 60 000 years, and the area where Darwin now stands is the country of the Larakia language group. Several unsuccessful British settlements had been made in the Top End before 1869, when the South Australian Government established Palmerston (renamed Darwin in 1911). Today's Darwin is Australia's gateway to Asia. Its residents are of many ethnic origins, and the city is impressively multicultural. The statue at left that celebrates Darwin's strong Greek connection stands in Smith St Mall.

SEEING DARWIN

Walking is a good way to see Darwin city and there are walking tracks along the Esplanade, Mindil Beach, East Point and the scenic northern suburbs foreshore. There are also extensive bicycle paths along open spaces. For an insightful tour, try the Tour Tub, that runs on an hourly circuit through the city, visiting points of interest. Buses depart from terminals in Darwin and the northern suburb of Casuarina.

Mindil Beach, site of many Darwin celebrations.

The Old Darwin Police Station and Courthouse (1884).

ALONG THE ESPLANADE

Bordered by Port Darwin and Bicentennial Park on one side and the city block on the other, the Esplanade runs south-east past major hotels, Lyons Cottage Museum and Old Admiralty House, then swings around between the Parliament House/Supreme Court/NT Library complex and Government House. The Old Police Station and Courthouse are further along the Esplanade while opposite, overlooking Darwin Harbour, is Survivors Lookout that recalls the World War II bombing of Darwin.

Darwin sunsets are particularly splendid during the Dry.

TEMP °C	J	F	M	A	M	J	J	A	S	O	N	D
MAX	32	31	32	33	32	31	30	31	32	33	33	33
MIN	25	25	24	24	22	20	19	21	23	25	25	25

Population: Approximately 79 000 (45.5% of the population of the NT)
Rainfall: Most falls from November to April, least from June to September.

Eating beside Darwin Harbour at the Wharf Precinct at the end of Stokes Hill Wharf.

An aerial view of the marina at Cullen Bay.

Stalls at popular Mindil Markets.

Fish come to Doctors Gully to be fed at high tide.

The MGM Grand Darwin Casino.

TYPICALLY DARWIN

Darwin's residents and visitors enjoy relaxing out of doors, especially during the Dry. The Wharf Precinct, at the end of Stokes Hill Wharf, is a great place to eat, with excellent seafood a specialty. Mindil Beach markets, held each Thursday evening in the Dry offer lots of things to buy, food from many nations and the chance to applaud a brilliant sunset. Sailing is a popular pastime, with a marina on the Cullen Bay development and clubs at Vesteys Beach, Fannie Bay. The 42-hectare Darwin Botanic Gardens offers tropical plantings and an Aboriginal Plant Use Walk. At the north-western end of the Esplanade, Doctors Gully is the venue for Aquascene, where schools of fish come to be fed every day at high tide.

MUSEUMS AND GALLERIES

The fine Museum and Art Gallery of the Northern Territory, about 4 km from the city centre at Fannie Bay, is a wonderful place to learn about life in the Indo-Pacific region. It has an impressive maritime section, and the exhibits featuring Aboriginal culture and art (*left*) and Top End wildlife are particularly fine. (Aboriginal art can be viewed, and purchased from, galleries in the city centre and at Stuart Park.) There is also a fascinating Indo-Pacific Marine and Australian Pearling Exhibition at The Wharf Precinct. North of Fannie Bay, the Military Museum at East Point Reserve displays mementos of World War II. Darwin Aviation Museum is on the Stuart Highway at Winellie, near the RAAF base and 8 km from the city centre.

SB

WHERE IS IT?

1	Doctors Gully	10	Ferry Terminal
2	Daly St	11	Lyons Cottage
3	Small Boat Harbour	12	Parliament House
4	The Esplanade	13	Stokes Hill Wharf
5	Bicentennial Park	14	Survivors' Lookout
6	Transit Centre	15	Wharf Precinct
7	Frances Bay	16	Government House
8	Smith St Mall	17	Lamaroo Beach
9	Pearling Exhibition	18	Port Darwin

The Great Egret, a billabong wader.

A Saltwater Crocodile displays its formidable teeth.

The Top End is the name often used for the northernmost part of the Northern Territory. It encompasses beaches, mangroves and tidal creeks (great fishing but take mosquito repellent), then coastal plains which, during summer's rains, become spectacular wetlands. From the plains rise the sandstone outliers and cliffs of the Arnhem Land Escarpment. This magnificent country is of great significance to its Aboriginal occupants and is home to abundant wildlife.

WILDLIFE ON VIEW

The Territory Wildlife Park is 60 km from Darwin, on the Cox Peninsula Rd near Berry Springs Nature Park. A four-km road, along which a shuttle passes every 15 minutes, loops around the exhibits. The Park has had notable success breeding native wildlife, especially birds, and the aviaries, which can be viewed from a raised walkway, are of great interest. Other fascinating displays include free-flying birds of prey, an excellent aquarium with an underwater walkway, an impressive nocturnal house, a wader lagoon and even feral animals such as camels and water buffalo.

Welcome
to the Territory
Wildlife Park

Opening Hours
8.30am - 4pm
Closed Christmas day only

Admission
Adults $12.00
Children $6.00
Pensioners $6.00
Family $30.00
(2 adults and 4 children)

The Antilopine Wallaroo is common across the Top End.

BIRDWATCHERS' PARADISE

There is always the chance of spotting a bird new to the Australian list in the Top End, and the coastal wetlands form magnificent bird habitat. Fogg Dam Conservation Reserve, 65 km from Darwin via the Arnhem Highway, is one of Australia's great birdwatching locations. A walking track gives access to monsoon forest and an elevated road leads across bird-rich wetlands to a two-storey observation deck.

The Comb-crested Jacana is common on Top End wetlands.

CROCODILES

The harmless Freshwater Crocodile and the dangerous Saltwater (or Estuarine) Crocodile are both found in the Top End wetlands and rivers. The possibility of a large "Saltie" being in residence should deter visitors from entering the water no matter how hot the weather. The model of a jumping croc at right stands near the Adelaide River, 67 km from Darwin, and its real relatives can be seen leaping for snacks from Adelaide River Queen Cruise vessels. A houseboat holiday on the Mary River reveals crocodiles in more natural occupations, usually basking on the banks or swimming quietly along. Farmed crocodiles can be viewed at Darwin Crocodile Farm, 40 km south of the city, and at Crocodylus Park near Berrimah.

Water lilies on Fogg Dam, a prime birdwatching spot.

KAKADU NATIONAL PARK

Nourlangie Rock and the Arnhem Land Escarpment.

Ubirr Stone Country.

Rock art at Anbangbang Gallery.

Jim Jim Falls.

Kakadu National Park lies 250 km from Darwin via the sealed Arnhem Highway. It covers 22 000 sq km and is managed by the traditional owners, the Gagudju people, and Parks Australia. This is a world of dramatic cliffs, massive sandstone outliers, billabongs covered with lotus lilies and birds, thundering waterfalls, extensive wetlands and rainforested gorges. The rocks harbour unequalled galleries of Aboriginal rock art, some of which are easily viewed at Nourlangie Rock. There are hotels at the town of Jabiru and at Cooinda, which is also the site of the Warradjan Aboriginal Cultural Centre. There are cruises on Yellow Water, near Cooinda. In the north of the park, there are superb rock art galleries at Ubirr and cruises are available on the East Alligator River. Helicopter and plane flights over the park take off from Jabiru.

A Jabiru.

Warradjan Cultural Centre.

Gagudju Crocodile Hotel, Jabiru.

Left inset: Exploring Yellow Water. *Main photo:* Yellow Water wetlands in summer.

A frill-necked lizard.

Bushwalkers will find many unspoiled places in Litchfield.

Magnetic termite mounds can be seen in Litchfield.

MAGIC LITCHFIELD

It is possible to drive the 115 km south from Darwin to Litchfield National Park, have a swim and a cold drink, then drive back to Darwin for lunch. However, it is worth taking time to discover the delights of the park, which include four beautiful waterfalls, the sandstone pillars called the Lost City and the remarkable north-south-oriented magnetic termite mounds.

Florence Falls cascade into a valley of monsoon forest in Litchfield National Park. The area has walking trails and picnic facilities.

The gorges of Nitmiluk National Park.

SOUTH FROM DARWIN

Pine Creek, 245 km south of Darwin on the Stuart Highway, was a goldrush town of the 1870s and has a museum with relics of the mining days. The Victoria Highway, from Western Australia, joins the Stuart Highway at the town of Katherine, 90 km further down the highway. Thirty km east is Nitmiluk National Park, whose scenic wonders include 13 gorges carved from sandstone by the Katherine River.

These red-walled gorges stretch for 12 km and are separated from each other by rapids. They may be explored on bushwalking trails varying in length from brief scenic walks to a testing five-day trek to Edith Falls. Many visitors prefer to view the park from vessels that cruise the gorges regularly during the Dry, but only set out when flood levels permit in the summertime Wet. Canoes, which allow views of gorge walls and wildlife, can be hired near the visitor centre (there is a Canoe Marathon each June).

Stock horses are brought into camp at the beginning of a working day on one of the Northern Territory's vast cattle stations.

Feeding fish on the Roper River, Elsey National Park.

Boab trees stand in a gorge in Gregory National Park.

ACROSS THE TABLELANDS

The vast plains that extend from the tropical Top End to the central deserts carry large pastoral leases. To the east of the Stuart Highway is the Barkly Tableland, to the west the Victoria River region. Gregory National Park, between the Stuart Highway and the WA border via the Victoria Highway, has rugged gorge and escarpment scenery and bushwalks that make it worth visiting.

The Roper River, 110 km from Katherine on the Stuart Highway, is the focus for Elsey National Park. A replica of Elsey Homestead, used in the film *We of the Never Never*, stands near Mataranka's thermal pool, a welcome respite from the dry northern plains.

SOUTH TO THE RED CENTRE

It's a long way from Mataranka down the Stuart Highway to Tennant Creek, though there are roadhouses at Larrimah, Dunmarra, Elliott and Renner Springs. At Threeways, 988 km south of Darwin, there is a memorial to the founder of the Royal Flying Doctor Service, John Flynn (his grave, *left*, is near Alice Springs, 537 km to the south). Tennant Creek is 26 km south of Threeways, near the site of a 1930s gold rush. About 100 km south again, beside the highway, is the Devils Marbles Conservation Reserve, known for its huge rounded boulders, some stacked in amazing and seemingly precarious piles.

The Devils Marbles, huge boulders of red granite that lie jumbled beside the Stuart Highway 100 km south of Tennant Creek.

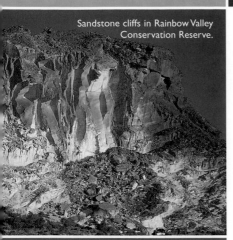

Sandstone cliffs in Rainbow Valley Conservation Reserve.

Central Australia is rich in historical associations. The Aboriginal ones stretch back many thousands of years, while others are more recent. Chambers Pillar (*right*) stands 160 km south of Alice Springs. To the Aboriginal people of the area, this sandstone tower represents a gecko ancestor of the Dreaming, Itirkawara.

The explorer John MacDouall Stuart was the first non-Aborigine to see this 30 m pillar on 6 April 1860, and those who followed him used it as a landmark. The forces of nature have created such magnificent monuments, and it is to be hoped that people who pass by will admire and photograph, but neither deface nor damage them.

The Old Telegraph Station, Alice Springs.

ALICE SPRINGS

An Overland Telegraph Line repeater station was established in 1871 near some springs, a permanent waterhole in the dry Todd River. The town of Stuart, founded nearby in 1888, was renamed Alice Springs in 1933. During World War II, The Alice became a major military base and the road north to Darwin was sealed to allow the transport of troops.

Modern Alice Springs can be viewed from the Alice Wanderer minibus, which runs every 70 minutes from 9 a.m. to 3 p.m. Other things to do in The Alice include taking an Aboriginal culture tour, seeing the desert from a hot-air balloon, visiting the Telegraph Station Historical Reserve, and riding a camel on a short trip or a two-day safari. Several Alice Springs galleries specialise in Aboriginal art.

A pool at Simpsons Gap, 22 km from Alice Springs.

EAST OF ALICE SPRINGS

Alice Springs stands in the middle of the MacDonnell Ranges, that stretch for 400 km across the centre of Australia. The parallel ridges of the ranges are slashed across by gorges carved by rivers that once flowed southwards into country that is now desert. The pools which still remain in these ravines are major attractions on any visit to the MacDonnells.

The Ross Highway leads east from the Stuart Highway just south of Alice Springs through the East MacDonnell Ranges. Highlights of a tour will be Emily and Jessie Gaps Nature Park, then, about 60 km from Alice Springs, the splendours of Trephina Gorge. Other attractions include N'Dharla Gorge National Park, Arltunga Historical Reserve and Ruby Gap Nature Park (site of a rush for "rubies" that turned out to be garnets).

Alice Springs Rodeo.

Trephina Gorge is in the East MacDonnell Ranges, 60 km from Alice Springs.

THE WEST MACDONNELL RANGES

The rugged parallel ridges of the West MacDonnell Ranges extend more than 150 km from Alice Springs. The ranges have a wealth of Aboriginal associations and their plants and wildlife are fascinating and varied. The marvellous scenery includes Ormiston Gorge and Pound and Serpentine, Redbank and Glen Helen Gorges. The Larapinta Trail runs along the ranges' crests and walkers can progress by easy stages to admire some of Australia's most imposing landscapes.

Right: The parallel ridges of the West MacDonnell Ranges. *Below:* Ormiston Gorge and Pound. *Below right:* Exploring Redbank Gorge.

The spectacular bluffs of Rainbow Valley are especially brilliant when highlighted by late afternoon sun after a desert thunderstorm has splashed them with rain.

Palm trees in Palm Valley, Finke Gorge National Park.

SOUTH OF ALICE SPRINGS

The James Ranges' scenic places include Finke Gorge National Park, 155 km from Alice Springs, whose unique palms survive from primeval times. Rainbow Valley is 22 km east of the Stuart Highway, and is best viewed at sunset. Watarrka National Park's spectacular Kings Canyon, one of the Centre's most picturesque areas, offers a variety of bushwalks and guided tours.

Kings Canyon, Watarrka National Park.

Kata Tjuta (the Olgas).

Learning about Uluru on a guided walk around the huge rock.

Fourteen Australian places are classified by UNESCO as World Heritage Sites. Uluru-Kata Tjuta National Park is eminent among them, and the red dome of Uluru has become an internationally recognised symbol of Australia. The park lies 470 km south-west of Alice Springs, in the south-west corner of the Northern Territory. The town of Yulara lies outside the northern boundary of the park and is reached by sealed road: many visitors prefer to fly to Yulara from the coastal cities or Alice Springs.

Uluru rises 348 m above the desert and is 3.6 km long and 2.4 km across. Two-thirds of it probably lies beneath the surface.

PHOTOGRAPHY

Sunrise and sunset bring to Uluru a series of photogenic colour-changes. There is a sunset viewing area halfway between Yulara and Uluru, but this is often crowded. However, with the aid of patience and a tripod, the camera or video can be set up and the photographer can wait for comparative solitude and, hopefully, a magnificent afterglow that will silhouette the Rock against fiery skies. The Anangu people ask that visitors do not photograph signposted areas of Uluru.

VISITING ULURU

It is a long way to Uluru, and it is well worth knowing something about the Rock before confronting it at close quarters. The Cultural Centre on the road from Yulara, 1 km from Uluru, describes the area, interprets the culture of the Aboriginal Anangu people who are the area's traditional custodians and discusses the national park that protects the area. A permit that secures entry to the park for five days can be obtained at Yulara or at the park gate. Remember that Central Australia is exceedingly hot during summer, while in winter the days are fine and nights can be cold.

Uluru is of significance to the Anangu people.

Climbing Uluru is against Anangu spiritual beliefs. The number of visitors making the taxing 1.6 km effort is diminishing.

Some of the many domes of Kata Tjuṯa.

KATA TJUṮA

Kata Tjuṯa, a group of gigantic sandstone outcrops, stands just over 30 km west of Uluṟu. The tallest of the domes, Mt Olga, rises nearly 200 m higher than Uluṟu. There are two walking trails, the longer of which takes explorers through the domes and the Valley of the Winds. The other trail visits Olga Gorge. There is a dune viewing area signposted between Yulara and Kata Tjuṯa, which gives a panorama of the dunes in the area and an overview of Kata Tjuṯa. There is also a Kata Tjuṯa Sunset Viewing Area situated several kilometres from the domes. The Aṉangu name Kata Tjuṯa means "many heads", and the domes are of great cultural significance. Photographers are asked not to take images of the Valley of the Winds, nor to single out Mt Olga as a subject, although the dome may be included in a general photograph.

DESERT LIFE

Desert plants and animals have many strategies for obtaining and conserving water. The animals often hide during the heat of the day and come out to feed at night. Some, like the Dingo, must drink water regularly, while others, like the rare Bilby, can get most of their water supply from their food. Desert reptiles may drink dew that has condensed on plants or their own skin. Desert vegetation is often protected by spines and hairs from animals and water loss. When rain falls, plants flower and seed prolifically, the seeds to await the next good rain to germinate.

Clockwise from top left: Spinifex Pigeon; Dingo; Thorny Devil; flowering Sturt's Desert Pea; Bilby; spinifex (Triodia).

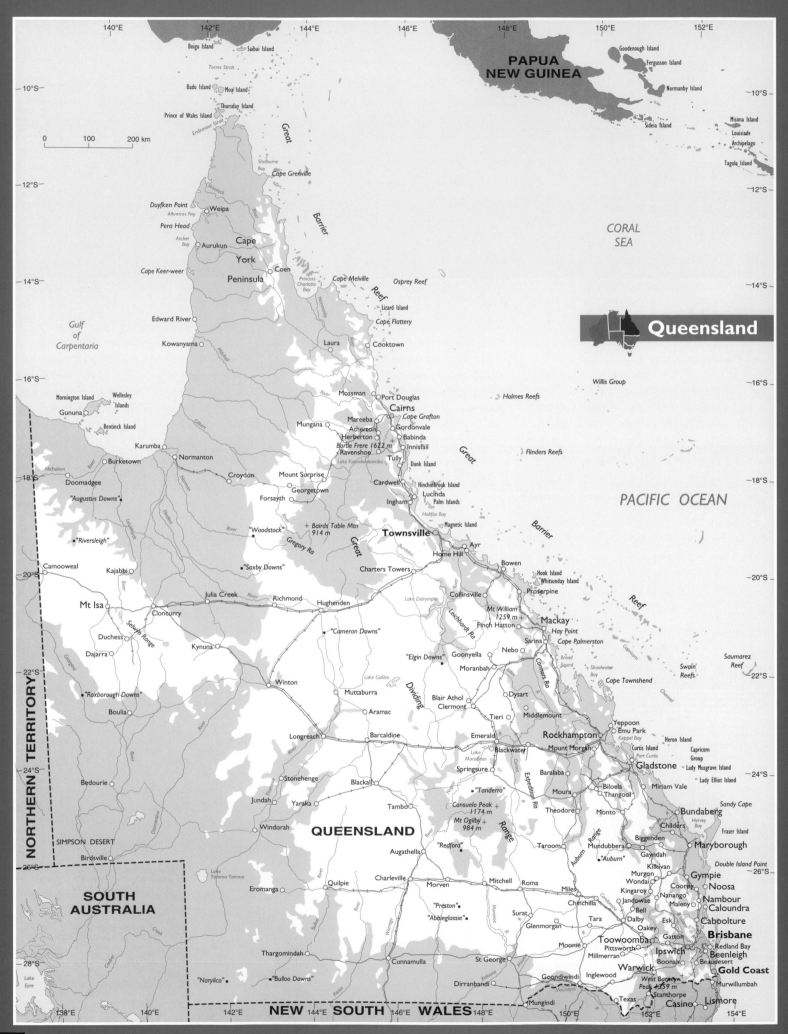

Queensland

PAPUA NEW GUINEA

CORAL SEA

PACIFIC OCEAN

NORTHERN TERRITORY

SOUTH AUSTRALIA

QUEENSLAND

NEW SOUTH WALES

Gulf of Carpentaria

Cape York Peninsula

Torres Strait

Boigu Island
Saibai Island
Badu Island
Moa Island
Thursday Island
Prince of Wales Island
Endeavour Strait

Duyfken Point
Weipa
Pera Head
Archer Bay
Aurukun
Cape Keer-weer
Coen
Edward River
Kowanyama
Shelburne Bay
Cape Grenville

Mornington Island
Wellesley Islands
Gununa
Bentinck Island
Karumba
Normanton
Burketown
Doomadgee
"Augustus Downs"
"Riversleigh"
Camooweal
Kajabbi
Mt Isa
Duchess
Dajarra
Cloncurry
Selwyn Range
Kynuna
"Roxborough Downs"
Boulia
Bedourie
Birdsville
SIMPSON DESERT
Lake Yamma Yamma
Lake Eyre

Croydon
Georgetown
Forsayth
Mount Surprise
"Woodstock"
"Saxby Downs"
Julia Creek
Richmond
Hughenden
"Cameron Downs"
Winton
Muttaburra
Aramac
Longreach
Barcaldine
Stonehenge
Blackall
Jundah
Yaraka
Windorah
Eromanga
Quilpie
Thargomindah
"Naryilco"
"Bulloo Downs"
Cunnamulla

Mossman
Port Douglas
Cairns
Cape Grafton
Mareeba
Gordonvale
Atherton
Babinda
Herberton
Bartle Frere 1622 m
Innisfail
Ravenshoe
Tully
Mungana
Lake Koombaloomba
Dunk Island
Cardwell
Hinchinbrook Island
Lucinda
Palm Islands
Ingham
Halifax Bay
Bairds Table Mtn 914 m
Magnetic Island
Townsville
Ayr
Home Hill
Charters Towers
Gregory Ra
Great Dividing Range
Burdekin
Lake Dalrymple
Collinsville
Bowen
Hook Island
Whitsunday Island
Proserpine
Mt William 1259 m
Finch Hatton
Mackay
Goonyella
Nebo
Hay Point
Sarina
Cape Palmerston
Moranbah
"Elgin Downs"
Connors Ra
Broad Sound
Shoalwater Bay
Cape Townshend
Blair Athol
Clermont
Dysart
Tieri
Middlemount
Emerald
Blackwater
Rockhampton
Yeppoon
Emu Park
Keppel Bay
Heron Island
Mount Morgan
Curtis Island
Capricorn Group
Springsure
Lake Maraboon
Baralaba
Gladstone
Lady Musgrave Island
Lady Elliot Island
Moura
Biloela
Thangool
Miriam Vale
"Tanderra"
Theodore
Monto
Consuelo Peak 1174 m
Mt Ogilby 984 m
Taroom
Mundubbera
"Auburn"
Bundaberg
Childers
Biggenden
Gayndah
Hervey Bay
Fraser Island
Sandy Cape
"Redford"
Augathella
Kilkivan
Murgon
Maryborough
Double Island Point
Charleville
Morven
Mitchell
Roma
Miles
Wondai
Kingaroy
Jandowae
Nanango
Gympie
Cooroy
Noosa
Maleny
Nambour
Caloundra
Surat
Chinchilla
Tara
Dalby
Oakey
Esk
Caboolture
"Preston"
Glenmorgan
Moonie
Toowoomba
Pittsworth
Gatton
Ipswich
Brisbane
"Abbieglassie"
Millmerran
Boonah
Redland Bay
Beenleigh
Beaudesert
St George
Warwick
West Barron Peak 1359 m
Gold Coast
Thargomindah
Cunnamulla
Dirranbandi
Goondiwindi
Inglewood
Stanthorpe
Casino
Mungindi
Texas
Murwillumbah
Lismore

Willis Group
Holmes Reefs
Flinders Reefs
Saumarez Reefs
Swain Reefs
Great Barrier Reef
Osprey Reef
Lizard Island
Cape Flattery
Laura
Cooktown
Cape Melville
Princess Charlotte Bay

Goodenough Island
Fergusson Island
Normanby Island
Misima Island
Sideia Island
Louisiade Archipelago
Tagula Island

0   100   200 km

102

QUEENSLAND

It is almost unfair to the rest of Australia for Queensland to be gifted with not only most of Australia's remaining warm-climate rainforest but the Great Barrier Reef as well. In this, the second biggest Australian State, more than 3 million lucky Queenslanders enjoy an abundance of blessings and are happy to share them with visitors from interstate and abroad.

Queensland's assets go far beyond rainforest and reef, and include beaches that stretch from the Gold Coast to Cape York, and World Heritage listed Fraser Island. The State capital is the lovely and lively city of Brisbane, and other centres well worth visiting include Townsville, Rockhampton, Cairns and Toowoomba. Explore west of the Great Dividing Range to discover the vast outback, where all of Australia's legends come to life.

BRISBANE & SURROUNDS

Brisbane City Hall and King George Square.

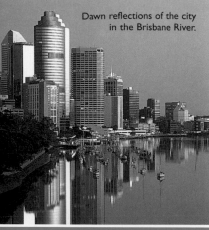

Dawn reflections of the city in the Brisbane River.

Brisbane City Hall and King George Square.

Brisbane's wonderful climate favours an outdoor lifestyle that has always been a hallmark of Queensland's capital. City and suburbs offer a multitude of courtyard restaurants, sidewalk cafés, riverside promenades and open-air events. The Brisbane River twines intimately about the city, and of recent years it has become a focus of entertainment and enjoyment. The splendid Riverside Centre and spectacular South Bank Parklands provide magnificent venues for public celebrations, weekend markets and family outings.

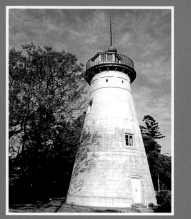

The Old Mill was erected in 1827.

THE BEGINNING

Brisbane was founded in 1824 as a gaol and convicts continued to work there until 1839. Free settlers were allowed to take up land after 1842. The Old Mill shown above was originally powered by convicts on a treadmill.

SEEING BRISBANE

Brisbane lies on the winding lower course of the Brisbane River, with seven bridges and a number of ferries linking northern and southern suburbs. The metropolitan area is webbed by bus and train services, with their hub at the Roma St Transit Centre.

For good views of the city and river, try the lookout platform in the Bell Tower of the Brisbane City Hall. Mt Coot-tha, 8 km west of the city centre, gives a magnificent view over the city east to Moreton Bay, south to the Border Ranges and north to the Glass House Mts.

For closer sightseeing, City Sights Trambus Tours shuttle past 18 city stops every day except Tuesday and there are plenty of bus day tours to features of interest around Brisbane. Cruises from Eagle St and other piers cover the river from its mouth to Lone Pine.

OPEN SPACES AND GREEN PLACES

Brisbane is a city of public parks and forest reserves, where outdoor activities abound – it is possible to abseil down Kangaroo Point Cliffs, on the riverbank opposite the city centre.

The City Botanic Gardens, at the southern end of the city block, and New Farm Park, between Fortitude Valley and the river, are popular with walkers and cyclists. Mt Coot-tha Botanic Gardens, 15 minutes by road from the city, includes many scenic walks.

Mt Coot-tha marks the start of the 28 500 ha Brisbane Forest Park, which can be explored on tours with themes such as rainforest, gold or nocturnal wildlife. Koalas (*above left*) and other animals star at Alma Park Zoo at Kallangur, 28 km north of the city via the Bruce Highway, and Lone Pine Koala Sanctuary, at Fig Tree Pocket, 11 km from the city centre.

Kodak Beach at South Bank Parklands, on the south bank of the Brisbane River.

TEMP °C	J	F	M	A	M	J	J	A	S	O	N	D
MAX	29	29	28	27	24	21	21	22	24	26	27	29
MIN	21	21	20	17	14	11	10	10	13	16	18	20

Population: Nearly 1 500 000 (45.7% of the population of Queensland)
Rainfall: All months of the year, but most falls from October to March.

The Riverside Centre stands between Eagle St and the Brisbane River. It is the venue for popular Sunday markets.

Outdoor café at the Performing Arts Complex.

The Tropical Dome at Mt Coot-tha Botanic Gardens.

New Farm Park in spring, when the Jacarandas bloom.

BRISBANE BY DAY

Queen St Mall is the heart of Brisbane's shopping precinct, and there are plenty of department stores, boutiques and specialty shops in streets and arcades nearby. City Hall has an Art Gallery and Museum, and just over the Victoria Bridge from the city centre are the excellent Queensland Art Gallery and Queensland Museum. Newstead House, a colonial mansion built in 1846, and Early-street Historical Village in Norman Park, are worth visiting to see how colonial Queenslanders lived. At the lively South Bank Parklands on the south bank of the Brisbane River, are restaurants, cafés, a safe swimming beach, South Bank Wildlife Sanctuary, rides on the Waterway Ferries, and places to picnic. The Visitor Information Centre is open daily.

BRISBANE AT NIGHT

There is a wealth of restaurants and nightclubs in the city centre. The Eagle St Pier, the nearby Riverside Centre, South Bank Parklands and suburbs such as Ascot, Paddington and Milton offer a variety of places to eat. Fortitude Valley is well-known for its eateries and clubs – Chinatown, with its many restaurants, can be found here. There are major cinema complexes in the city and suburbs, and these and other entertainments are advertised in the *Courier Mail* newspaper. Live theatre can be seen at the Performing Arts Complex, South Brisbane. The club scene comes alive in Petrie Terrace and, for the adventurous, in Fortitude Valley. The Treasury Casino (*above left*) is a sumptuous complex overlooking the river.

WHERE IS IT?

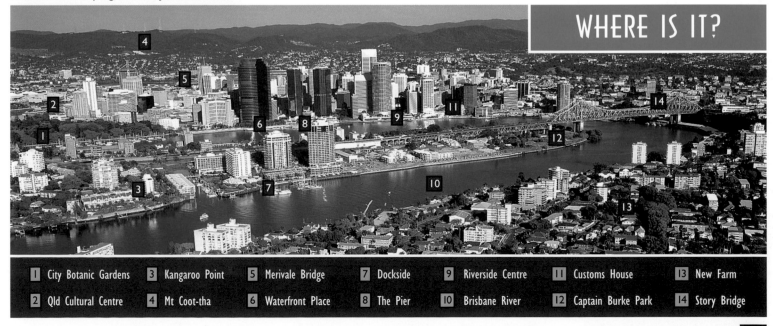

1 City Botanic Gardens	3 Kangaroo Point	5 Merivale Bridge	7 Dockside	9 Riverside Centre	11 Customs House	13 New Farm
2 Qld Cultural Centre	4 Mt Coot-tha	6 Waterfront Place	8 The Pier	10 Brisbane River	12 Captain Burke Park	14 Story Bridge

Relaxing at Surfers Paradise on the Gold Coast.

THEME & FAUNA PARKS

The Gold Coast's theme parks and wildlife sanctuaries provide an embarrassment of choices. Sea World, just north of Surfers Paradise, features live dolphin and sea-lion shows plus many other attractions. The highlights at Dreamworld, 17 km north of Surfers, include Tiger Island (*right*) and thrilling rides. Movie World re-creates a film studio. Wet'n'Wild focuses on water-sports.

Fleay's Wildlife Park, West Burleigh, offers fascinating fauna and interesting walking tracks. Currumbin Sanctuary attracts colourful parrots to feed morning and afternoon, as well as displaying wildlife. Eight km up the beautiful Currumbin Valley is Olson's Bird Gardens, where native and exotic birds can be seen in impressive garden settings.

THE GOLD COAST

The most popular holiday destination in Australia, the Gold Coast stretches more than 40 km from the mouth of the Coomera River south to the Queensland/New South Wales border. This international resort is one hour south of Brisbane by road and is serviced by an airport 20 km south of Surfers Paradise, near the border town of Coolangatta.

A Gold Coast holiday can be as simple or as sophisticated as the holiday-maker wishes. There is a huge range of places to stay, places to eat and things to do, from swimming, surfing and fishing to dining, night-clubbing, shopping and taking in a show at Conrad Jupiters Casino. The Gold Coast is in festive mode for the IndyCarnival each March, the Surfers Paradise International Triathlon in April, and for the Magic Millions Summer Racing Carnival held at Bundall, just west from Surfers, in January.

Sea World is one of the Gold Coast's major attractions.

Raptis Plaza is an opulent shopping complex at Surfers.

Feeding Rainbow Lorikeets at Currumbin Sanctuary.

The view south from above The Spit, along Main Beach and Surfers Paradise. At right is the Broadwater.

Conrad Jupiters Casino at Broadbeach.

THE GOLD COAST HINTERLAND

Rainforest, Lamington National Park.

The Gold Coast hinterland offers a magnificent alternative to sun, sand and togetherness. On the Queensland–NSW border, in the McPherson Ranges (an outlier of the Great Dividing Range that was once part of a huge volcano) it is possible to find solitude and some of nature's loveliest sights. Close to Brisbane, Tamborine Mountain's nine small national parks protect forests and waterfalls and its small towns offer delightful art and craft galleries. Lamington National Park is a gem in the crown of south-eastern Queensland. Its rainforests, spectacular cliffs, waterfalls and abundant wildlife can be enjoyed through 160 km of walking tracks. Twenty-four km apart via the Border Walking Trail, Green Mountains and Binna Burra are popular places to stay, each with a camping ground and accommodation. A Binna Burra bus operates from Surfers Paradise, while Green Mountains can be reached by bus from Brisbane Transit Centre or the Gold Coast.

Australian King-Parrot.

Elabana Falls, Lamington National Park.

A pair of Sugar Gliders.

The town of Springbrook is about 30 km south of Mudgereeba and is a good jumping-off point from which to visit Springbrook National Park. Highlights of the park are waterfalls, walking tracks, swimming areas and Natural Bridge, where glow-worms star at night.

The Numinbah Valley.

Natural Bridge, Springbrook National Park.

From Bribie Island, the view across Pumicestone Passage can include sunset behind the Glass House Mts.

HEADING NORTH FROM BRISBANE

The Bruce Highway runs north of Brisbane through country that was once coastal heathland, with tracts of rainforest where streams flow to the sea from the Great Dividing Range. Much is now farmed or otherwise developed. The Glass House Mts, 60 km north of Brisbane, were named by Captain Cook in 1770 and are favourites with climbers, bushwalkers and picnickers. Reach them via the Old Bruce Highway, now called Glass House Mts Rd. The coastal town of Caloundra looks across the northern entrance to Pumicestone Passage which divides the mainland from Bribie Island, a popular place for holidays and day trips.

The Bruce Highway bypasses many towns, but they and tourist attractions are clearly signposted. The Big Pineapple (*left*) is just off the highway near Nambour, about 100 km north of Brisbane. To the east, on the coast, are popular resorts Maroochydore and Mooloolaba, home to the excellent aquarium Underwater World. There is a fast motorway north to Noosa, but the road that follows the coast passes through pretty beach-side towns. The Noosa area is a holiday-maker's mecca with great beaches, the river, Noosa National Park, smart shopping and eating. To the north is the rainforest, beaches, lakes and waterways of the Cooloola section of Great Sandy National Park.

Nectar-eating birds like this Scaly-breasted Lorikeet are common in coastal heathlands.

A view across Coonowrin, other peaks of the Glass House Mountains and the coastal plain to the sea.

Mooloolaba is noted for good fishing and excellent sailing.

Maroochydore is on the estuary of the Maroochy River.

Eateries and art galleries abound in Maleny.

ARTS, CRAFTS AND MARKETS

The pleasant climate of the Sunshine Coast hinterland, especially in the mountains that parallel the coast, and the beauty of the country have brought artists and craftspeople to settle around towns such as Montville, Maleny, Mapleton and Kenilworth. Combine a visit to the Sunshine Coast with a tour through the green hinterland, visiting galleries, looking at the scenery and enjoying the relaxed lifestyle.

Saturday markets are held at Eumundi, north of Nambour.

From McCarthy's Lookout, near Maleny, farmlands and forest remnants stretch to the Glass House Mts.

Baroon Pocket Dam, between Maleny and Montville.

PARKS AND LAKES

The Sunshine Coast offers countless opportunities for exploration by water, by road or on foot. Noosa National Park has good walking tracks. To the north, the Great Sandy National Park covers 54 000 ha of lakes, heathlands, forests and coastline between Noosa and Rainbow Beach, and is ideally viewed from a cruise on the Noosa River. Lake Cooroibah and Lake Cootharaba, both on the river, offer camp sites, accommodation and, in the case of the former, camel safaris as well. A drive along the crest of the Blackall Range from Maleny to Mapleton offers magnificent views across the coastal plain.

The Noosa River (*top centre*) leaves the mountains and lakes and winds to the sea past the resort town of Noosa.

Fraser Island, 190 km north of Brisbane, is the world's largest sand island, 120 km long by 15 km wide, with some dunes rising to 200 m. Much of the island is covered with vegetation, including rainforests growing along creeks running down to the sea. There are around 200 lakes on the island, which was placed on the World Heritage List in 1992. The northern half of the island is included in the Great Sandy National Park.

One of Fraser Island's famous Dingos.

ENJOYING FRASER

Vehicles and passengers can be ferried to Fraser Island from the mainland from Inskip Point, near Rainbow Beach, from River Heads and from Urangan Boat Harbour. Kingfisher Bay Resort also transfers visitors to and from the island, and it is possible to fly from Hervey Bay.

A permit is needed to take a vehicle onto the island, and a 4WD vehicle is the only way to traverse the many sand tracks and beaches. Drivers should keep in mind that the island is easily damaged by careless driving, and that vehicles are easily damaged by salt water. Highlights of a Fraser trip should include visiting some of the lakes (McKenzie and Wabby are amongst the best), admiring the coloured sand cliffs at Cathedral Beach, surfing on an ocean beach and exploring a rainforest creek such as Wanggoolba.

A view across Fraser Island, showing perched lakes, awesome sand dunes and unspoiled beach.

FRASER'S BIRDS AND BEASTS

Fraser Island is rich in wildlife, including Dingos that roam the island at will (and which should not be fed by visitors). There are more than 230 species of birds, including the fish-eating White-bellied Sea-Eagle (*left*), and in spring the heathlands are bright with flowers. The perched lakes (formed in dunes above the water-table) have their own fauna, including freshwater turtles and rare Rainbow Fish.

Wanggoolba Creek winds through rainforest.

The dramatic cliffs of Indian Head.

WHALE-WATCHING FROM HERVEY BAY

Hervey Bay, about four and a half hours by road from Brisbane, is well serviced by buses and tours. Between Maryborough and Bundaberg, protected by Fraser Island, 5 townships stand on the Bay: Point Vernon, Pialba, Scarness, Torquay and Urangan. Hervey Bay is an ideal place for a safe swimming and fishing holiday. Between late July and mid-October, whale-watching cruises run from Urangan  Boat Harbour (*right*). Humpback Whales (*below*) voyage from the Antarctic to the warm waters of the Great Barrier Reef to give birth. Cruise boat operators are careful not to alarm the giant mammals. A popular Whale Festival is held in Hervey Bay each August.

TYPICAL OF QUEENSLAND'S COAST

The Queenslander, a wooden house raised high off the ground, with a corrugated iron roof and wide verandahs. It is built to cope with heat, heavy rain and termites.

Mangroves grow in salt or brackish water along beaches and estuaries, their seedlings entrusted to the tides. They anchor sand and mud and shelter fish fry and other life.

Sugar cane grows on the fertile coastal plain – watch out for harvesters (*above*) and cane-trains. Sugar products include table sugar, hardboard, stock feed and rum.

THE GREAT BARRIER REEF

The Reef and some of its myriad fish.

THE LIVING REEF

The Great Barrier Reef is a wonderland of wildlife, both marine and terrestrial. Many of the Reef's most popular attractions — for example, breeding colonies of seabirds such as terns (*inset*) and nesting sites of marine turtles — are vulnerable to human interference. Observe them with respect and from a distance.

Scuba diving — a close look at the Reef.

The framework of the Great Barrier Reef is made up of the limestone shells built by countless tiny coral animals (polyps) to protect their soft bodies. This World Heritage listed marvel stretches for 2000 km up the coast of Queensland from near Bundaberg to Torres Strait. It includes approximately 2500 reefs, 250 islands that were once parts of the mainland, and 70 coral cays big enough to have been given names.

Enjoying the Tropical North Queensland lifestyle.

ISLANDS AND RESORTS

Some people prefer to visit the Great Barrier Reef islands on day trips from mainland bases such as Gladstone, Cairns or Port Douglas. Others make a longer stay on one of the Reef's many islands (there are resorts on about 20, and it is possible to camp on many islands). It is worth some research to find the resort that suits your requirements, such as serious scuba diving (*right*) or non-stop organised entertainment.

The southern islands of Lady Elliot and the Capricorn-Bunker Groups are accessed through the mainland ports of Bundaberg and Gladstone. Heron Island, 72 km east of Gladstone, is a nesting place for turtles. It is particularly popular with snorkellers and scuba divers, and can be reached by helicopter or barge.

Great Keppel Island, 13 km off the coast, can be reached by plane from Rockhampton or by ferry. It is a family resort with splendid beaches. The magnificent Whitsunday group (see also p. 114) consists of around 70 scenic continental islands, whose mainland jump-off points are Airlie Beach and Shute Harbour. Magnetic Island, popular for its beaches and bushwalks, is 8 km from Townsville. Off the coast from Tully, in North Queensland, are beautiful Dunk and Bedarra Islands, the former with a world-famous resort. Further north, off Cairns, are Green and Fitzroy Islands, both popular with day-trippers. Another day-trip destination, the Low Isles, are off-shore from Port Douglas. The northernmost resort island is Lizard, 240 km north of Cairns and only 15 km from the outer edge of the Reef.

There are tours to reefs and islands, and the Great Barrier Reef Marine Park is ideal for scuba diving or snorkelling (*inset*).

ENJOYING THE REEF

On the Reef, as elsewhere in Australia's wild places, the old adage "look but don't touch" is a good one to follow. Coral cuts are slow to heal and some Reef denizens sting or bite in self-defence. However, the most dangerous element of the Barrier Reef for most people is the sun. A hat, a long-sleeved shirt and plenty of sunscreen are Reef essentials.

Exploring the wonders of a coral outcrop, also known as a bommie.

The Lionfish has venom-tipped spines on its back fins.

On a day-trip to the outer Reef.

Some coral fish. *Top left and clockwise:* Emperor Angelfish; Pink Anemone Fish; Ringtail Cardinalfish; Harlequin Tuskfish.

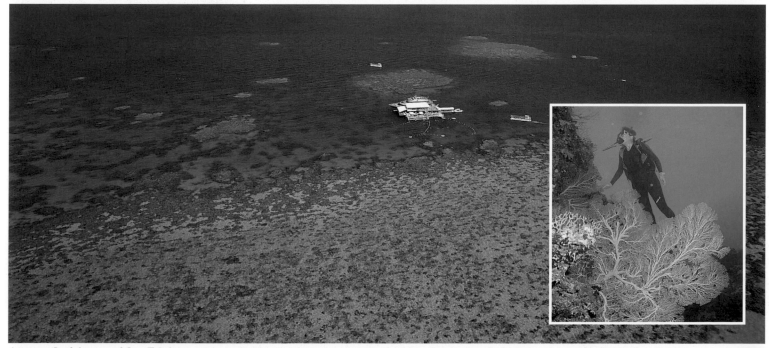
Agincourt Reef, due east of Cape Tribulation, can be explored on a day trip on a catamaran from Port Douglas. *Inset:* Scuba diver and gorgonian fan coral.

A Green Turtle hatching.

TURTLE TALES

Six of the world's seven species of marine turtles live and nest in Queensland. Females come ashore between November and February to lay their eggs in the sand of beaches at Mon Repos, near Bundaberg, and on the Capricorn-Bunker Group of islands and the Capricorn Coast.

A nesting female is afraid of bright lights, sudden movements and deep-toned sounds, and will abort her attempt to nest if too disturbed. She is particularly wary when crawling up the beach and digging the pit in which she will lay her eggs. Baby turtles (*right*) are distracted from their dash to the ocean by bright lights and movement. They need every bit of luck they can get — only one in every 1000 will survive to breeding age!

Boating in the Whitsundays.

Two popular regions of the central coast of Queensland are known as the Capricorn Coast and the Whitsunday Coast. The Capricorn Coast stretches from Gladstone north to Sarina, its major centre the city of Rockhampton. Offshore, the Capricornia section of the Reef includes Lady Elliot Island and the Capricorn-Bunker Groups.

North of the Capricorn Coast, the Whitsunday Coast focuses on the Whitsunday Islands, 74 continental islands with fringing reefs. In 1770, Captain Cook described the Whitsunday Passage as "one continued safe harbour", and bareboating, (hiring a craft to sail around the Whitsundays) is an ideal way to enjoy this magnificent area.

Rockhampton's elegant Commercial Hotel houses the popular Heritage Tavern and Flamingo Nightclub.

ROCKHAMPTON

The major city of the central Queensland coast, Rockhampton stands on the Tropic of Capricorn and is situated 40 km up the Fitzroy River. Gold and copper discoveries at nearby Mt Morgan in the 1880s have left a legacy of elegant historic buildings in "Rocky". Today, beef cattle are the district's major product. The Rockhampton Art Gallery is well worth visiting, and the Berserker Range to Rockhampton's north offers picnic grounds and guided tours of cave systems.

Whitehaven Beach is one of the Whitsundays' loveliest spots.

THE WHITSUNDAYS

There are resorts on seven Whitsunday islands and camping is allowed on some of the group. Proserpine and Mackay are the largest nearby centres and boats leave from Airlie Beach and Shute Harbour. Planes and helicopters fly to some islands from Whitsunday Airport, and Heli Reef flies from there to Fantasea's Reef World, a pontoon on the outer reef.

Hill Inlet, Whitsunday Islands National Park.

Townsville stands on Cleveland Bay, overlooked by Castle Hill.

TOWNSVILLE, REEF CITY

Townsville, third largest city in the State, is a university city, an armed forces city, and the port for north Queensland. It is a city of some sophistication, home to the Sheraton Breakwater Casino and a top class marina. At the Great Barrier Reef Wonderland, marine life can be viewed from a walk-through tunnel. The Omnimax Theatre shows films about the Reef and there is a Museum of Tropical Queensland. The Town Common Environmental Park is famous for wetlands birds such as the Brolga (*inset above*). The delights of Magnetic Island are just 8 km offshore, and there are flights and tour boats to the Reef and other islands.

Hinchinbrook Island is 390 sq km in area and includes dramatic granite mountains (Mt Bowen is 1120 m high), bordered by extensive beaches on the eastern or ocean side and mangroves and forests on the mainland aspect. The northern end of the island is reached by ferries via the town of Cardwell, while the southern end is accessed via Lucinda. Hiring a boat or a houseboat is a great way to see Hinchinbrook, while the 23 km Thorsborne Trail takes walkers from Ramsay Bay to George Point. All of Hinchinbrook is a National Park.

Hinchinbrook Island, with Missionary Bay in the foreground.

Whitewater rafting on the Tully River.

TULLY AND MISSION BEACH

The town of Tully, nestled in the Great Dividing Range beneath 678 m Mt Tyson, has an average of around 4200 mm of rain per year. The Tully River, which rushes from the mountains to the Coral Sea, is famous with whitewater rafters, and Tully is a good base for rapids adventures and exploring the mysteries of the rainforest.

There are a number of settlements along the beautiful 14 km of tropical sand that is the Mission Beach area. The Wet Tropics Visitors Centre is at the northern end of Mission Beach next to the Tourist Information Centre. Just offshore from Mission Beach are Dunk and Bedarra Islands. Dunk, a hilly and rainforested island 4.5 km from the mainland, has a large resort and is popular for day trips. It is accessible by water taxi and cruises. Bedarra is the site of a charming, and exclusive, resort.

A White-lipped Tree-frog.

Fortunately situated in the centre of some of the most scenically beautiful and ecologically remarkable areas in the world, Cairns is the stepping-stone to marvels. It is also a city of great charm and character, and its buildings reflect both its history and the modernity that enables it to welcome visitors of all nationalities. The Atherton Tableland, just a short journey up the ranges away, offers rainforests, rolling farmlands and delightful towns.

The Cairns Birdwing, one of Far North Queensland's lovely butterflies.

CAIRNS, TROPICAL CITY

The "capital" of Far North Queensland is the centre of a network of tourist drawcards such as the Reef, the rainforest and the Atherton Tableland. It is also an interesting place in its own right, with a relaxed, tropical lifestyle that does not end at dusk, plenty of places to eat and shop, and a number of attractions.

Visitors should walk along the Esplanade and see the wading birds that feed on the foreshore (below), visit the popular Pier Marketplace, enjoy the weekend Rusty's Markets, stroll through the Flecker Botanic Gardens and take in an exhibition at the Tank Arts Centre nearby.

Marlin Marina and the Pier Marketplace, Cairns.

Reef themes decorate the busy Pier Marketplace.

OFF TO THE BARRIER REEF

Near Cairns, the Great Barrier Reef lies comparatively close to the coast, and a multitude of Reef-oriented activities begin on the stretch of Trinity Inlet between Marlin Marina and the Wharf Cruise Liner Terminal. There is something for everyone in the many options offered – dive courses, day-trips to the outer Reef and cruises of varying lengths to the Reef and a variety of islands.

Two islands have particularly good day-trip facilities. Green (left), a coral cay 27 km north-east of Cairns, offers a good swimming beach, trips in glass-bottomed boats, and the gallery, museum and aquarium of Marineland Melanesia. Fitzroy, 26 km south-east of Cairns, has good snorkelling beaches and Reefarm, where giant clams and pearl oysters are bred. There are diving day-trips to a number of reefs and to Michaelmas Cay.

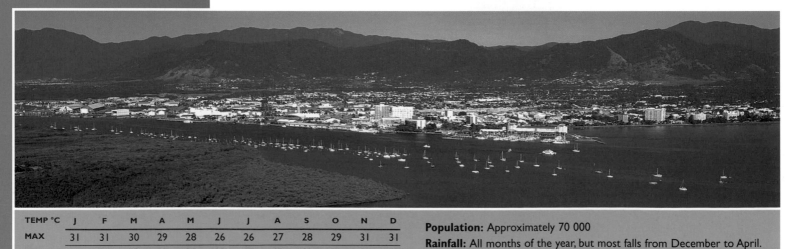

TEMP °C	J	F	M	A	M	J	J	A	S	O	N	D
MAX	31	31	30	29	28	26	26	27	28	29	31	31
MIN	24	24	23	22	20	18	17	18	19	21	22	23

Population: Approximately 70 000
Rainfall: All months of the year, but most falls from December to April.

Cairns, seen over Trinity Inlet and looking westwards to the Atherton Tableland. *Inset:* Some Cairns climatic data.

A Skyrail gondola on its way up the MacAlister Range.

Kuranda Markets, held Wednesday to Friday and Sunday.

Tjapukai Aboriginal Cultural Park dancers.

The Scenic Railway passes Stoney Creek Falls (*above*) as well as giving a good view of the Barron Falls, near Kuranda.

THE ATHERTON TABLELANDS

There are several ways to travel from Cairns to Kuranda, a picturesque village in the rainforest on the edge of the Atherton Tablelands. Kuranda Scenic Railway winds up the range through 15 tunnels and over 40 bridges, past waterfalls and through rainforest. The Skyrail gondolas, high above the forest canopy, carry passengers from Caravonica Lakes near Cairns 7.5 km to Kuranda with two sightseeing stops along the way. Caravonica Lakes is also the site of Tjapukai Aboriginal Cultural Park, which presents indigenous culture in a way that combines Dreamtime folklore with modern technology.

The Tablelands can be seen by driving along a circuit beginning and ending in Cairns. South-west of Kuranda, 37 km along the Kennedy Highway, is Mareeba, known for coffee, macadamia nuts, tobacco and cattle (the Mareeba Rodeo is held each July). To the south, the Tablelands' main town, Atherton, lies near Lake Tinaroo. Yungaburra, 13 km east of Atherton, is notable for its massive Curtain Fig and is near Lakes Barrine and Eacham. Malanda is a dairying town 20 km north of beautiful Millaa Millaa Falls (*above left*). Crawfords Lookout gives another sightseeing opportunity before you travel north through Babinda to Cairns.

Josephine Falls, in Wooroonooran National Park, in the ranges west of the Bruce Highway between Cairns and Innisfail.

A rainforest stream.

RAINFOREST WONDERS

Australia's northern rainforests are relics of a time when the continent was far wetter than it is today. Rainforest grows only where there is high, regular rainfall, and is home to a bewildering variety of animals. Some of them, such as the Southern Cassowary, are found only in the wet tropics rainforest of far north Queensland. Its remarkable plants include many which are medicinally useful as well as ornamental (see the beautiful Cooktown Orchid, *inset right*).

Alive with animals, birds and butterflies, its buttress-trunked trees and stream-bed rocks embroidered with lichens and mosses and decorated with orchids, the rainforest is one of the world's wonders.

Port Douglas is an international tourist destination set in the midst of scenic beauty, within easy reach of two World Heritage attractions, the Great Barrier Reef and the wet tropics rainforest. This charming town is just off Highway 1, and is reached by one of the most picturesque coastal drives imaginable. North of Port Douglas is the largest surviving area of unlogged rainforest left in Australia. North again, Cape York Peninsula provides travellers with a challenge that brings rich rewards in the discovery of wildlife and wild places.

Heading for the Low Isles, a coral cay crowned by a lighthouse.

PORT DOUGLAS

From Port Douglas, 65 km north of Cairns, it is easy enough to visit Mossman Gorge or Cape Tribulation, or to cruise the Daintree River. However, Port Douglas itself offers plenty of entertainment, including shopping at Marina Mirage, eating at excellent restaurants, shopping at Sunday's Anzac Park Markets, visiting Rainforest Habitat, going on horseback treks, or sailing off Four Mile Beach. Ben Cropp's Shipwreck Museum is just along the pier.

TRIPS TO THE REEF

There are several places in Port Douglas that conduct scuba-diving courses, and a number of Great Barrier Reef tours are available. One of the most popular trips is by fast catamaran to Agincourt Reef, on the outer Reef. Such a day trip allows visitors to snorkel, and to see the underwater world from a semi-submersible or from an underwater observatory. Other possibilities are helicopter rides, and, for certified divers, scuba diving.

On Four Mile Beach, just south of Port Douglas.

The Rainforest Habitat at Port Douglas.

A horseback trek along the beach near Port Douglas.

THE WET TROPICS WORLD HERITAGE AREA

Queensland's Wet Tropics World Heritage Area includes rainforests stretching from Townsville to Cooktown. The forests of the Daintree-Cape Tribulation area (*above*) contain stands that have never been logged. The Australian Rhododendron (*above right*) and the Daintree River Ringtail Possum (*right*) are examples of the unique plants and animals to be found in this wilderness.

NORTH TO COOKTOWN

The town of Daintree, 36 km north of Mossman, marks the end of the fully sealed highway, and the ferry across the Daintree River is a gateway to adventure. A cruise is a good way to see the river and surrounding country. It is 34 km from the ferry to Cape Tribulation and, unless it's the height of the wet season, a family sedan can travel the distance. There are also flights, sea cruises and tours by road from Cairns to the Cape. It is possible to push on to Cooktown along the Bloomfield Track in a 4WD, but many drivers prefer to cover the 332 km from Cairns to Cooktown along the inland Peninsula Development Road.

Cape Tribulation is one of the rare places in Australia where the rainforest runs right down to the sea.

The tip of Cape York, the northernmost point on the Australian mainland.

CAPE YORK PENINSULA

It is 952 km from Cairns to the tip of Cape York Peninsula along the most direct route, the Peninsula Development and Telegraph Roads. The trip can be made in a conventional vehicle in the dry season, but is best in a 4WD, essential for visiting many attractions. It is best to travel as early in the Dry as possible, for roads deteriorate as the season passes and many are impassible in the Wet. There are road tours to the Cape that visit interesting places along the way, and it is possible to fly in to Weipa, Coen, Lockhart River (Iron Range) and Laura. Pajinka Wilderness Lodge, at the very tip of the Cape, can be reached via Injinoo Airport near the town of Bamaga.

CENTRAL & WESTERN QUEENSLAND

Lawn Hill, an oasis best reached by 4WD vehicle.

The area of Queensland that lies west of the coastal strip is huge, and these pages highlight only a few of its many outstanding aspects. It is a land of sometimes violent contrasts: mountain ranges rise from treeless plains; droughts parch the landscape before floods bring new green life. Drive through Queensland's outback realising that beauty is sometimes concealed in the vastness – for example, Lawn Hill National Park, 100 km west of Camooweal to Burketown road, is a pristine pocket of gorges and tropical plants.

THE BUNYA MOUNTAINS

The Bunya Mountains National Park is about 230 km west of Brisbane, between Dalby and Kingaroy. The Bunyas are outliers of the Great Dividing Range, and rise to more than 1100 m. The national park is named for its Bunya Pines and it also contains rainforest and eucalypt forest. Among its multitude of bird species is the Australian King-Parrot (*right*). It's a wonderful place to camp and walk.

PASTURELANDS AND FARMLANDS

The fertile Darling Downs stretch west of the Great Dividing Range. They were early divided up for pasture and grain growing, and towns like Toowoomba, 128 km west of Brisbane, are rich in historic buildings. Of particular interest are the Jondaryan Woolshed, 45 km west of Toowoomba and the Historical Village at Miles, 166 km further along the Warrego Highway.

The Granite Belt, a plateau to the south of the Downs, is a district of fruit orchards and vineyards, which sell their excellent products at the cellar door and hold a Spring Wine Festival.

Lake Nuga Nuga, a gem not far from Carnarvon Gorge.

CARNARVON GORGE NATIONAL PARK

One of Australia's most magnificent scenic reserves, Carnarvon National Park, is 720 km north-west of Brisbane via the towns of Roma and Injune. The final 45 km of the road is unsealed and may become impassable after rain. The Carnarvon Gorge section of the park features a creek running between dramatic sandstone cliffs, deep pools bordered with palms and ferns, and a lovely Moss Garden. Many sections can only be reached by a lengthy walk, but the surroundings and the wildlife are well worth the effort. The Mt Moffat part of the park is far more rugged. Carnarvon National Park is rich in Aboriginal art and archeological sites.

The Stockman's Hall of Fame and Outback Heritage Centre, 2 km from Longreach along the Barcaldine road.

Major Mitchell's Cockatoo.

THE OUTBACK TRADITIONS

Much of central Queensland's plains country supports large herds of cattle and flocks of sheep, whose survival often depends on water pumped from the Great Artesian Basin by windmills. The contribution of the pastoral industry to Australia is celebrated in the fine Stockman's Hall of Fame and Outback Heritage Centre at Longreach, which is about 1200 km from Brisbane and 700 km from Rockhampton. Barcaldine, 108 km east of Longreach, is the home of the impressive Australian Workers Heritage Centre. Hughenden, 243 km south-west of Charters Towers on the Flinders Highway, is a cattle and sheep town 65 km south of spectacular Porcupine Gorge National Park.

In Porcupine Gorge, "a little Grand Canyon".

SOUTH-WEST QUEENSLAND

Cooper Creek country during drought.

The south-west of Queensland, known as the Channel Country, is a desert for much of most years. However, heavy wet season rains falling on northern Australia may send flood waters down the network of rivers and creeks that lead into the Lake Eyre basin in South Australia. The Channel Country regenerates as the floods dry up and cattle are hastily moved onto the new pastures for fattening. Boulia is the main centre of the Channel Country, but tiny Birdsville (population 100) is famous for its remoteness and its September race meeting.

A harsh but fragile country.

The famous Birdsville Hotel.

An Emu deep in grass after rain.

THE BEST SEASON FOR A VISIT

THE VEHICLE & DRIVING

Check vehicle, accessories and spare parts before departure. Keep vehicle to the left, especially around corners and over crests. Slow down on unsealed roads. Watch out for straying stock and wildlife.

THE PEOPLE IN IT

Always carry water and, if necessary, food and extra fuel. Drink frequently, but avoid alcohol. On a long trip, stop and relax or change drivers every 90 minutes. By law, all occupants must wear a seatbelt.

BACKSEAT NAVIGATORS

Kids can help plan the route, navigate if they can read, or spot road signs if they can't. Take things for them to do and healthy snacks for constant consumption. Toilet-train them pre-trip.

REMEMBER...

Thorough planning avoids most disasters. Do not drive through dust. Pass a road train only if the road is clear for 1 km ahead. Before entering water, check depth, force and hidden obstacles.

1 Gardens across southern Australia. Visit in spring for flowers, autumn for leaves.

2 Whitewater rafting. Year-round on Tully River, Queensland, elsewhere check with operator.

3 Waterfalls, northern Australia. Best flow during summer Wet, November-March.

4 Whale-watching. Humpback Whales eastern and western coasts, late July-mid October. Southern Right Whales along southern coast June-October.

5 Wildflowers, Western Australia. August-October. Kings Park Wildflower Festival held October.

6 Central Australia. Best time to visit is May-October. High daytime temperatures November-April.

7 Canberra festivals. Floriade is held each October, Canberra Festival each March.

8 Australian Alps and High Country, NSW/Vic. Visit during winter for snow sports, during summer for walking, fishing and other activities.

USEFUL ADDRESSES AND TELEPHONE NUMBERS

TOURIST OFFICES

Australian Capital Territory Tourist Commission, Level 13 Saphouse, Bunda & Akuna Sts, Canberra 2601 (tel. 1800 026166 toll-free or 06 205 0044/ 205 0666)

Canb. Visitors Centre www.canberratourism.com.au

New South Wales Tourism, 11–13 York St, Sydney 2000 (tel. 13 20 77)

Northern Territory Tourist Commission, 43 Mitchell St, Darwin 0801 (tel. 08 8999 3900)

Queensland Government Travel Centre, Adelaide & Edward Sts, Brisbane 4000 (tel. 13 18 01)

Far North Queensland Promotion Bureau, Grafton & Hartley Sts, Cairns 4870 (tel. 070 513 588)

Tourism South Australia, 1 King William St, Adelaide 5000 (tel. 08 8303 2033 or 1 800 882 092 toll-free)

Tasmanian Travel Centre, Elizabeth & Davey Sts, Hobart 7000 (tel. 03 6230 8233)

Tourism Victoria, Visitor Information Centre, Town Hall, Melbourne 3000 (tel. 03 9790 3333/9650 1522)

Western Australian Tourist Centre, 469 Wellington St, Perth, WA 6000 (tel. 1 300 361 351)

ACCOMMODATION

Backpackers Resorts of Australia (head office), 25 Lavarack Ave, Eagle Farm Qld 4009 (tel. 07 3268 5733)

Bed & Breakfast Australia (head office), 666 Pacific Hwy, Killara NSW 2071 (tel. 02 9498 5344)

Youth Hostels of Australia, (head office), 422 Kent St, Sydney NSW 2000 (tel. 02 9261 1111)

Farm holidays: contact telephone numbers
  Australian Farm Host Holidays 060 298 621
  Northern Territory 1800 621 336
  Queensland 07 3361 2390
  South Australia 08 8892 2755
  Tasmania 03 6224 1612
  Victoria 03 9650 2922
  Western Australia 097 263 912

* All addresses and telephone numbers on this page are subject to change. If problems arise, check address and contact number in current telephone directory for city.

MOTORING CLUBS

There is an automobile association in each Australian State and Territory. When driving anywhere in Australia, it is useful to be a member of one of these organisations, for each organisation is affiliated with the Australian Automobile Association, and when interstate a member of any organisation can request services from the local body.

Some of the popular facilities offered are emergency breakdown assistance, vehicle towing and vehicle inspection services. Other services include tuition in safe and defensive driving, motor vehicle insurance cover and advice as to approved repairers. Extremely useful membership benefits include advice about motoring holidays and tours. This can consist of maps, guides, reports on road conditions, travel bookings, concessional rates for accommodation and car hire, and other services.

Club, or social, membership allows the use of club facilities and accommodation.

AAA Australian Automobile Association, 212 Northbourne Ave, Braddon Canberra, ACT 2612 (tel. 06 247 7311)

AANT Automobile Association of the Northern Territory, 79-81 Smith St, Darwin, NT 0800 (tel. 08 8981 3837)

NRMA National Roads & Motorists Association, 151 Clarence St, Sydney, NSW 2000 (tel. 02 9260 9222) or 92 Northbourne Avenue, Canberra, ACT 2601 (tel. 13 21 32)

RAA Royal Automobile Association of South Australia, 41 Hindmarsh St, Adelaide, SA 5000 (tel. 08 8202 4600)

RACQ Royal Automobile Club of Queensland, 300 St Pauls Tce, Fortitude Valley, Qld 4006 (tel. 07 3361 2444)

RACT Royal Automobile Club of Tasmania, cr Patrick & Murray Sts, Hobart, Tas 7001 (tel. 03 6232 6300)

RACV Royal Automobile Club of Victoria, 550 Princes Hwy, Noble Park, Vic 3174 (tel. 13 19 55)

RACWA Royal Automobile Club of Western Australia, 228 Adelaide Tce, Perth, WA 6000 (tel. 08 9421 4444)

NATIONAL PARKS

Environment Australia, (head office) Tobruk House, 15 Moore St, Canberra, ACT 2601 (tel. 06 274 1111)

Australian Capital Territory Parks & Conservation Service, PO Box 1119, Tuggeranong, ACT 2901 (tel. 06 205 1233)

New South Wales National Parks & Wildlife Service, 43 Bridge St, Hurstville, NSW 2220 (tel. 02 9585 6444)

Parks & Wildlife Commission of the Northern Territory, Frances Mall, Palmerston, NT 0830 (tel. 08 8999 4500)

Parks Australia North, GPO Box 1260, Darwin NT 0801 (tel 08 8946 4300) (Uluru information tel. 08 8956 2299; Kakadu information tel. 08 8938 1120)

Queensland Department of the Environment, 160 Ann St, Brisbane 4000 (tel. 07 3227 8187)

Great Barrier Reef Marine Park Authority, 2-68 Flinders St, Townsville, Qld 4810 (tel. 07 4750 0700)

Department of Environment & Natural Resources, 77 Grenfell St, Adelaide, SA 5000 (tel. 08 8204 1910)

Department of Environment & Land Management, 134 Macquarie St, Hobart, Tas 7000 (tel. 03 6233 8011)

Parks Victoria, 378 Cotham Rd, Kew, Vic 3101 (tel. 03 9412 4795)

Department of Conservation & Land Management, 50 Hayman Rd, Como, WA 6152 (tel. 09 9334 0333)

EMERGENCY!
IN ALL STATES FOR POLICE, AMBULANCE AND FIRE-BRIGADE
DIAL 000

Publisher's note: While every effort has been made to ensure that the information in the book is accurate at the time of going to press, things change and the Publisher cannot accept responsibility for errors or omissions. Steve Parish Publishing welcomes information and suggestions for corrections and improvements from readers.

Once journeys are over, recollections of places and experiences gradually fade. The traveller who photographs (or videos) scenes during a holiday will be able to turn the pages of memory for years to come. While it is fun to record what happened to loved ones along the way, as in the image at right, scenic treats such as the Boab tree at sunset shown at the left should not be ignored. In most parts of Australia, the prettiest light occurs early in the morning and late in the afternoon, so journeys to scenic wonders should be planned to allow some photography at those times.

Happy occasions can be captured in shots like this one.

BUYING A CAMERA

A 35 mm single lens reflex camera body with an 80-200 mm zoom lens can be used for landscape and people shots and for photographing wildlife in sanctuaries and parks. For the best landscape pictures, especially those taken in low light, the use of a tripod is essential. It need not be heavy, but it must hold camera and lens steady. Camera and lens should suit the purpose — a good rule is to buy the best quality the budget will allow, then take very good care of it.

This Cape York scene was taken on print film. The other images in this book were taken on transparency film.

FILM HINTS

It is cheapest to buy film in bulk before setting out on a trip. If it is necessary to renew supplies along the way, purchase it from air-conditioned premises, keep it (and the camera) cool while travelling and have it processed as soon as possible after exposure.

Print (negative) film is easy to buy, to process, and to place in albums to give lasting records of journeys. Transparency (positive) film is more expensive to buy, has fewer processing outlets, is not as easy to use, but is favoured for reproduction by many publications.

MAKING THE MOST OF THE LIGHT

1 Uluru, late afternoon.　　2 Uluru, an hour later than 1.　　3 A view of Adelaide taken in full sunlight.　　4 The same view of Adelaide photographed at dusk.